Seven Days
with Him

By: **Sandra Kay Gigandet**

Dedication

This book is dedicated to my dear mother, Rebecca Jackson, who loved God more than life itself. She passed away on August 9, 2022.

I wish she'd lived to see me complete this book, but even though she didn't, I'm sure she would have been proud of me. Knowing this gives me the courage to continue doing what I love.

Thank you, Mom, for your love and support throughout the years. I will always love you.

Table of Contents

Introduction

Everything about him was perfect: his tall, dark body, kind words, pleasing-to-the-eye looks, and a smile to die for. He was perfect, one in two million! What woman wouldn't want him?

The funny thing was that my gut was saying something different; I should have listened!

Day One

The first time I saw him was on Saturday, October 22, 2000, at a singles party. My best friend, Liz, invited me to get me out of the house. Although I wasn't into that kind of thing, I agreed to get her off my back.

We agreed that she would pick me up, and we'd drive over together around eight p.m. I spent all day shopping for the perfect outfit, as I wanted to look good, considering I hadn't been out in that setting in years. Liz called me at noon to see how things were going; things were okay, I guess, I told her.

"You will be all right; look at the bright side, you will meet many men tonight," she said.

"Right, who needs them?" I replied.

Let me explain. I was in a relationship years ago with a man I thought I would spend the rest of my life with. When I met him, I was a Junior, and he was a Senior. We had what I would call a great relationship. Jacob was a kind and intelligent guy; he played football and baseball and was quite attractive. We spent all our free time together. On weekends, we would go to the park to watch the older couples, who held hands and showed a great deal of love for each other. Sitting back and watching them was a joy; it always gave us hope for a great future together.

Three years passed before we knew it, and that's when I noticed things started to change. He started canceling our dates, and even though he didn't call to cancel that day, I'm guessing he must have decided that he didn't need to warn me that he wouldn't be coming around anymore.

He was supposed to meet me at my parents' house for Christmas dinner, but he never showed up. I was worried sick, not knowing what happened to him. We waited for hours to hear from him, but we never heard a word the rest of the evening. After waiting for what seemed like a lifetime with no word, I called his parents to see if they could tell me anything. They said he had left their house hours ago to come to my parents'. After finding out he never made it, they were worried. We began calling everyone we could think of to see if we could find anything that might explain his behavior or his whereabouts. We called the Hospitals, the Police, all of his friends, and mine, but none of them had seen or heard from him. The day passed with no word, and my heart feared the worst. I found it difficult to rest or sleep, not knowing what had happened to him.

Later that night, I received a call from a friend I hadn't called, who told me she had seen him earlier in a different city with a girl she didn't know. She said they hugged, kissed, and held hands. My heart sank! How could he? I was so worried, and he was out with another girl on Christmas Day! I could not believe it. Not my Jacob! Not the nice, sweet, intelligent, loving young man I knew. Why was this happening? Was it true? Was Jacob out with another girl? Is this why he never showed up? This couldn't be true, I told myself over and over again. Something else must have happened. Tracie could not have been telling the truth. As far as I was concerned, that was not Jacob's nature. I never, in all the years of knowing him, saw any signs of deceit. But now? I was unsure what to believe. If true, how would we continue this relationship? If it was not true, where was he?

The following day, he called to set up a dinner date to explain why he hadn't shown up for Christmas dinner. There was no excuse or apology, and he acted as if nothing had happened. He picked me up later that evening for dinner. We were noticeably quiet on the trip to the restaurant. He had nothing to say, I thought to myself. He looked straight ahead, never looking at me. He pulled up in front of the restaurant, parked the car, and got out. Walking up to the door, he started to walk in as if he were alone. He had always opened the car door for me; he was always a gentleman, opening every door we entered, but not tonight. This was strange.

I got out and hurried up to the door as he went in. It was like I wasn't there. He did not hold it open for me, and it almost shut on me. I had to catch it! What was going on? This was not like him, not like him at all. I walked behind him, trying to keep up. He walked quickly and looked straight ahead. I was concerned that something was wrong. He didn't look back; he just walked ahead with no concern for me.

He asked for a table, and then we were seated. After sitting there for a while, I wondered if he had spoken to his parents this morning. I decided to ask him if he had, and he said he had got in late the night before and didn't want to wake them. He did not see them or anyone else before he left home, he said.

I sat and waited for him to say something else, but he didn't. I waited for a while longer, but he never said anything. Then I asked him why he'd asked me to dinner. Before he could answer, I said, "Tell me why you did not show up for Christmas dinner, and it better be good!" So many thoughts ran through my mind as he stared off into space. He never apologized for not coming, and he always gave an excuse for why he canceled, but not this time. He said nothing.

I thought about Tracie and what she'd told me. He sat, looking off in the distance, while we waited for our waitress to take our order. Trying to be patient, I asked him how his day was going, and he replied that it was going well, perhaps even better than well. The more he talked, the more I realized he was probably lying. I had only come to dinner to hear his excuse, and I was upset that I had to open my car door and pull out my seat from the table. I sat looking at him; he was always looking in a different direction. Why wasn't he looking at me?

"What did you do today?" I asked.

"Not too much," he said.

"The appointment you had earlier, did you make it on time?" I asked.

"I did," he replied.

I had to coax a conversation out of him. Then he told me he had another appointment later that evening and couldn't miss it.

"You've had a lot of appointments lately. What's going on?"

"Nothing. Work stuff," he answered, not looking at me.

"It must be tiring I said.

"Not really," he replied.

We ordered our food as he looked at his watch. I felt like a fool! Why was I sitting there? Maybe I just wanted to hear the excuse he would give me for missing dinner. Or perhaps I was crazy. The thought of what Tracie said kept running through my head: I saw him kissing, hugging, and holding hands with another girl. I couldn't get that thought out of my mind; it played on a loop repeatedly. Ask him about what Tracie said, I kept telling myself while waiting for him to explain.

Finally, the waitress brought the food. Looking at him, I chewed my food slowly. Then I said sarcastically, "Why didn't you show up for dinner last night?"

He barely turned his head and said, as I explained to you on the phone, "I had a family emergency."

"What was that emergency?" I asked.

He looked upset at me and said, "Mother was not feeling well; I decided to stay home with them. I forgot to call because of everything that was happening."

Was that it? Was that the best he could come up with? That only made it worse and caused me to blow my stack! His mother was sick. That puts the icing on the cake. I at least thought his dog might have gotten run over! Or his brother and his wife might have had their baby. But his mother was sick? Please! What a bold-faced lie! He wasn't as intelligent or honest as I thought he was.

"What was wrong with your mom?" I asked.

"Nothing much, just tired from the weeks before, trying to prepare everything for Christmas."

If he repeated the word "nothing again," I thought I would punch him right in his lying mouth. Everything was nothing! By this time, I was so mad that I couldn't see straight.

Ask him about the girl. Tell him what Tracie said. Tell him and see if he lies about it, I thought. I mustered enough courage and said, "I know your mother wasn't sick. I spoke to them yesterday when you didn't show up. They told me you left their house hours before I called them to see what happened to you. You would have known this if you had talked to them this morning instead of running out to see her!"

For the first time since we'd been there, he looked me straight in the face and asked, "Who are you talking about? Who is she?"

"Jacob! I know all about her! You were out with another girl on Christmas, and I know about your hugging, kissing, and holding her hand! How could you? We were a couple. We discussed getting married, having a family, and how we would grow old together. How could you do this to us? I was hoping it was all a lie. But now I know it's the truth. Tracie was right, you are cheating on me! And you have the nerve to sit across from me and act as if you've done nothing wrong. Why didn't you have the courage to tell me it was over? And you still haven't said anything? Must I drag it all out of you? You could have told me you were unhappy with me. I've been a good, faithful partner and would have never cheated on you. You are not the man I thought you were. I have nothing more to say to you. You are a liar and a cheater, and I don't want you. You can go back to your girlfriend and leave me alone!"

I stood up and said, "Nothing will ever happen between you and me again! Get it? Nothing!"

When I left, my heart was broken. Water flowed down my face like I was in a shower. Tears flowed uncontrollably; I had never hurt so much. The man I was to marry was no longer in my life. The man I was to marry was a liar and a cheater. Even now, I didn't want to believe it, but I knew it was true.

That day, I decided to stop dating and stay away from any relationship that could cause me pain.. I never wanted to be hurt again, so I was hesitant when Liz asked me to go to the singles party.

Around seven-thirty, Liz called to see if I was ready to go, and reluctantly, I said yes. I thought about Jacob again, hoping no one would notice me at the party. I would sit back in a corner somewhere out of sight and hope no one would see me. I wished I could become invisible.

Liz arrived around seven forty-five, and we arrived at the church at eight sharp. I exited the car and looked down at myself. Liz saw me looking and assured me I looked gorgeous. I looked down at myself again and thought, I did look pretty good, if I must say so myself. We ran our fingers through our hair and went in. The room was decorated beautifully; the colors were red and white, reminiscent of Valentine's

Day. I'm guessing they must have wanted the room to feel like a haven of love.

The room was full of young and old singles, more ladies than men; many of them already appeared to have hooked up. Liz introduced me to some of her other friends, and then, there he was, sitting in the corner, just like I said I would do. I took a second look, and, for some reason, all my senses went numb. He looked gorgeous and shy, and it was apparent he was not looking for a date.

Liz touched me on the shoulder and asked if I had seen something I liked.

I shook my head and said, "Really, Liz!"

"That's a new person who has only been attending church for two months," she said.

"What's his name?" I asked.

"I'm not sure, but he seems shy and quiet like you."

I wondered why he was sitting in the corner. The way he looked, I couldn't understand why he wasn't mingling with the others.

I couldn't take my eyes off him; this was strange. After Jacob, I'd never paid men much attention, but now I couldn't keep my eyes from following him. Everything about him was perfect! He was perfect, with his tall, dark body, kind words, pleasing looks, and a smile to die for. What woman wouldn't want him? He was one in two million, and right now, I wanted to be the one to get his attention, or so I thought. I felt strangely out of place; this was not like me at all.

Sitting and watching him for a while, I watched as he stood up and walked in my direction. Oh, my goodness! It scared me to think he might see me in the corner. I did not want to be seen, I told myself. Is he coming over here? I was unsure but hoped so. What would I say to him? I hadn't talked to anyone like that in years, and I wished I wouldn't make a fool of myself tonight and turn him off. God, please let me say the right things. Do not let me make a fool of myself to a total stranger, I asked.

He came over and said hello. I almost shuddered! He introduced himself as Aiden Summers. He reached out his hand to me, and I shook it. Then something strange happened, I felt a surge of energy throughout my body.

"My God, what's happening?" I pulled my hand away quickly. "Hello, I'm Alex Smith, and it's so lovely to meet you."

"I hear you're new to the area?"

"Yes, I am. I've only been here for about two months," he replied. I told him he'd love it here.

"So far, so good," he said, smiling. "I let a friend talk me into this."

"You too! I replied. "My friend Liz invited me, and I didn't want to come, but she insisted, so here I am."

"I'm glad you came. I didn't think I would meet anyone here tonight," he said.

"I'm happy I came too," I told him with a smile. "Would you like to sit down?" I asked.

"Sure. Please tell me what you do around here for fun," he asked.

"Well, I haven't had too much fun lately. I work a lot, I'm always busy, and life always has something for me to do."

"Are you busy all the time? And do you not have time to enjoy yourself occasionally?" he asked.

"No, not really. I've had so much to do for the last two years, trying to keep busy."

"Why are you so busy?" he asked.

"It's a long story, and I'd rather not talk about it if you don't mind."

"No problem. So, tell me how long you've known Liz?" he asked.

"It seems we've known each other for a lifetime. We attended preschool together; our parents were best friends. Liz and I grew up together, and we lived next door to each other. I guess I've known her for as long as I can remember. She's my best friend.

"Wow! That's a long time. I don't mean you're old or anything. I'm saying you've known each other for a long time, since you were in preschool."

"Yes, we have, and I wouldn't have it any other way. She's been a big help to me and is always there when I need her. I try to be as good a friend as she is."

He smiled again. As I looked at him, his smile seemed to change; it didn't look the same. Something was different. I closed my eyes and then reopened them quickly, looking at him again. Everything was fine. I thought it must have been my imagination.

"Would you like something to eat or drink?" he asked.

"Yes, I'll take some punch if you don't mind.

He stood up and walked toward the punch table. I called Liz over to ask if she saw him talking to me, and she said, "Yes, you seemed to be having a good time for someone who didn't want to come." I looked at her and smiled, then said, "His name is Aiden Summers, and I think he likes me."

"What should I say to him? So far, he's asked all the questions."

"Alex, just be yourself. If you're yourself, he can't help but like you. Stop freaking out, girl, you've got this." I looked around and saw he was returning.

"Liz, you can go now, he's coming back."

"Relax, Alex. You'll be all right. Remember what I told you: be yourself. You can't go wrong."

I ran my fingers through my hair and took a deep breath. I was so nervous. "Calm down, what's wrong with you?" I asked myself. I hadn't felt this way before, not even when I first met Jacob. This felt different. I'm not myself; something was different. I wasn't sure what it was, but something felt wrong.

As I waited for him to return, I saw that he took a detour to a smaller punch table, picked up a second glass of punch, and returned. He handed me a glass, and I sipped the punch.

"This is tasty, a combination of pineapple and Sprite! It's fruity. I love pineapple in everything," I said with a silly grin.

"Pineapple and Sprite! That's it!" he yelled. "I was trying to figure that out. I can't believe you got it on the first sip. You seem good at figuring things out."

"I try when I need to," I replied.

"That's good. You never know when you'll need to figure something out he said."

I looked at him a little confused and said, "I guess."

Looking at my watch, I realized it was much later than I had imagined. It was almost three a.m. Wow! The time had flown by, and we were having such an enjoyable time that I didn't realize how late it had gotten. Looking around for Liz, I saw that she was talking to someone I didn't know.

"Would you please excuse me, Aiden? I need to speak to Liz briefly."

"Of course. I'll wait right here until you return," he replied.

I walked away toward Liz. She looked at me and smiled.

"Are you ready to leave yet?" I asked.

"Yes," she replied.

"Then why didn't you tell me? It's almost three a.m., and you have to work later this morning."

"Well, you were having so much fun. I didn't want to be the one to rain on your parade," she said.

"Liz, you're so silly sometimes. Just let me say goodnight to Aiden, and I'll be right back."

Walking over to him, I noticed he was watching me strangely. He smiled, and again my heart melted.

"We're leaving now. It's late, and Liz has to work in a few hours," I told him.

We said our goodbyes, he said he understood, then added, "It was so lovely meeting you, and the conversation was great." I smiled, said thanks, turned, and walked away. Then I heard him call my name.

"Alex! Can I see you later this evening?"

I stopped in my tracks and slowly turned around. I had been waiting for him to ask me out all night, but he didn't. Thinking he wasn't interested, I forgot about it. Now he's asking, and I was so excited.

I looked at him with a smile and said, "Yes." Where that yes came from, I don't know. It was as if someone else answered for me.

"I would be happy to share my number with you so you can call me with the details."

He took my number and gave me that breathtaking smile again. My heart melts whenever I see it.

"I will contact you later to provide you with the details," he said.

"Okay," I replied, then turned around and walked out with Liz.

"It seems like you like him, and he is into you," Liz said. "Yes, it does seem that way. I never thought I would feel this way about a guy again, but believe it or not, there are things about him that I love."

"What are they? What do you love about him?" she asked. "I love his wonderful smile and the way he looks out for me. He is always polite. I love to look at him, he is perfect," I told her.

"Perfect? No one is perfect, Alex. Do this for all the right reasons, not because you love looking at him," she said.

"You are right, Liz. I'll make sure it's for all the right reasons."

We walked to the car and headed for my house.

"Alex, are you ready for a relationship?" She reminded me that I hadn't dated in years, how it requires a lot of time and energy, and how it could take a lot out of you.

"Liz, I know you're right. I'm unsure how this will work out, but I like him."

"Alex, just be careful. We know very little about him. We just met him," she said.

I turned and looked out the car window. All I could think about was Aiden.

Liz dropped me off in front of the house, and we said goodnight. I went inside, kicked my shoes off, and sat on the couch. It had been a very long day, and I needed some rest, but all I could think about was his smile and kindness. It would be a long night. I went upstairs, got ready for bed, and then it hit me. Unexpectedly, my stomach began to ache. It was in knots, and I began to feel a strange sensation, one that was very unsettling. Something was wrong. Again, I could not put my finger on it, but it was. Ignoring my stomach, I pinched myself to ensure I was not dreaming when it came to Aiden. Things were looking up for me, and I was happy about it.

Day Two

I woke up tired, not wanting to get out of bed, and I realized I had overslept. It was afternoon. I pulled the covers back over my head; last night had been hard on my body, and I was not used to staying up so late. My head hurt, and I hadn't eaten since the previous day. Thinking back on all I had to do, I decided to get up. I dragged myself out of bed and sat on the edge of it for a few minutes; it made me feel so tired thinking about everything that needed to be done; my life was nothing but work.

I am always tired and never rested. I dragged myself off the edge of the bed and bent over to stretch my back; for some reason, it felt like it was broken. I pulled my legs, arms, and everything else I could. Today was going to be a hard one; walking downstairs, I felt so hungry that I went into the kitchen to see what I could find. Looking in the fridge, I couldn't find anything to eat. I realized I had had no time to go grocery shopping, so I shut the fridge door and walked away.

Walking over to the couch, I decided to rest for a few more minutes. I dropped my head into my hands and asked God to help me accomplish all the things I needed to do that day, as I often did. Then, I headed back upstairs to get ready.

My bed looked good to me, but there was no way I could get back into it. I needed a shower, and I only had hours before I had to get ready for my date. I didn't know yet what time it would be, but I did know he would call soon with the details, and I knew I had slept half the day away. I'd forgotten how exhausting relationships could be; I hadn't been in one for over two years. It's only been one night, and

I'm already feeling stressed. I hope he was worth it, I told myself. Jumping in the shower. It felt wonderful, and I began to loosen up a little; not wanting to get out, I stayed in for a while longer. Everything was moving in slow motion. I couldn't get moving this morning; ignoring my body and everything else, I got out of the shower, dressed, and then headed downstairs to find the perfect outfit for the evening.

Opening the door to leave, the phone rang; I stopped, turned around, put my keys back on the table near the front door, and asked myself if I should answer. It could be work calling to see if I would come in for someone who's calling out. Lately, that's been happening a lot, but Aiden did say he would call, so I decided to answer it, praying it was him. To my surprise, it was!

"Hello, may I speak to Alex?" he asked.

"This is she," I replied.

"Hi, did I wake you?"

"No, I've been awake for a few hours."

"That's good. I wanted to give you time to sleep in. You were up late last night, and I wanted you to rest. I told you I would call to provide you with the details for tonight."

"Yes, you did. What do you have in mind?" I asked.

"We would have dinner at my place if I'm not being too forward. I know we just met, and if you don't feel comfortable, we don't have to," he said.

"That's fine with me. I would love to have dinner with you at your place. Text me your address, and I'll be there," I replied.

"No way! There's no way I'm letting you drive yourself. I'll come and pick you up at 7 p.m., if the time is okay with you."

"The time is fine. Do I need to bring anything with me?" I asked.

"Just you. All I need is you, Alex. Nothing else."

He made me smile.

"If you're sure, I'll be ready at 7."

We said goodbye, and I hung up the phone. Picking up my keys again, I headed to the car.

I stopped by a little dress shop that was out of my price range; it was expensive, and I only had a few dollars to spend. What I needed was a miracle; I needed the clearance rack! And to my surprise, they had one. It didn't take long for me to spot the dress of my dreams; it had a yellow top, black at the edge of the hem, a strap on the left shoulder, and was made of silk, falling just above the knees. I tried it on, and it flowed beautifully! It looked great on me; I figured I could rock this dress to the max. He should love this, I thought. And the price was within my range. Now, to find some shoes. I paid for the dress and some accessories, then rushed out to find the perfect shoes to go with it.

Last night, my feet hurt from the shoes I wore to the singles party; it was all I could do to keep them on. But not tonight! I am getting shoes that will not hurt my feet. Walking into the shoe store, I noticed they were having a big sale! Just what I needed. I found a beautiful pair of black stilettos. I must admit they were a little higher than I would typically wear or buy, but I wanted to impress Aiden. I paid for them, then headed to the grocery store to pick up a few things I needed. It took me a while to shop, as I only had a few bucks to spend. I had to pick my items wisely.

I returned to the car with the groceries and looked at my watch. I only had an hour and a half to get ready for tonight. I broke a few traffic rules while driving home. I should pay more attention to time. Now I'm rushing again! This was my life story! Rush! Rush! Rush!

Arriving home, I quickly parked, jumped out, and opened the door. Running inside, I almost fell. Rushing into the kitchen, I put away the frozen food and refrigerated items, leaving the rest for later. Then, I ran back outside to the car to get my dress and shoes. Running upstairs, I dropped the bag with my shoes, and it fell back down the stairs.

"I don't have time for this!" I thought.

I ran back down, grabbed the bag, and ran back up. I laid everything out on the bed and jumped into the shower. I felt as if I had worked a double shift.

Time passed faster than I could move! I found myself getting irritated in the shower, so I quickly washed myself and jumped out. Looking at the clock, I only had forty-five minutes to finish up everything, then wait for Aiden. My hair was wet, and I didn't have the time to do anything special to it; all I could think of was to blow it dry and flat-iron it. That was the best I could do. Anyway, my hair looked nice when it was flat-ironed, so I did that and got dressed. I looked at myself in the mirror and thought about what Aiden had said at the party. He said, "You seem to be good at figuring things out," and looking in the mirror, he was right; I looked good. Everything I bought brought out the best in me.

I stared a while and smiled.

"You did well today, girl! Just don't make a fool out of yourself tonight. Just be you, like Liz said, and everything will be all right."

I was good at figuring things out when I needed to, I thought. I smiled again. These things I had not thought about in years; now, suddenly, my head was full of thoughts I had forgotten about years ago. Spending time with Aiden last night brought back both fond and bittersweet memories. After getting dressed, I picked up my shoes and headed back downstairs. When I reached the bottom of the stairs, I realized I had left my purse, jacket, and keys upstairs. Shaking my head, I headed back up to get them.

"You would forget your head if it weren't attached to your shoulders," I thought.

Slowly walking back downstairs, I began to think of Jacob. What was it about me that caused him to cheat? What did I do? Or what didn't I do? What caused him to be so dishonest and unfaithful? I had always loved him; I was faithful, and I was a pretty girl, not the prettiest in the world, but not the ugliest, I thought.

I went downstairs and sat. The doorbell rang. I got up and went to the door.

"Who is it?" I asked. "It's Aiden," he replied.

I opened the door, and he stood with my favorite-colored flowers.

"Are those for me?" "Yes, they are."

"Thank you, Aiden. I'll put them in water; it won't take long. I'll be right back."

As I put the flowers in the water, my stomach began to feel uneasy again; I almost dropped the vase. I could feel a presence there that I'd never felt before. I grabbed my stomach and bent over, hoping it would feel better soon, and it did. That was the second time this had happened. Not thinking much about it, I finished the flowers and returned to the door. He was still standing in the same spot as I had left him.

"I'm ready now, let's go."

"Don't forget your coat, purse, and keys lying on the table over there," he reminded me.

I smiled, turned to get them, and walked out with him. He helped me down the steps, opened the car door, made sure I was inside, fastened my seatbelt, and shut the door. I sat there wondering, as he walked around the car, did this happen? Did he do all those things for me? I couldn't believe it. I pinched myself to ensure I wasn't dreaming, and it hurt badly, so I knew I wasn't.

He got in, put on his seatbelt, and started the car. We took a detour, stopping at a grocery store along the way. He went in and came out with only one bag. He held it like a bottle. I didn't mind the stop; I was with him, and that's all that mattered. He got back into the car, and then we were off again. It didn't take long to arrive at his house. He lived closer to me than I realized, but I'd never seen this house before, and I had been all over this town since I was a young child. How could I have missed something so big and beautiful?

Looking at it, I felt baffled; it was strange that I had never seen it before, and it was mind-blowing. He parked the car, got out, and approached my door. Opening it, he reached for my hand. I was scared to touch him. I remembered the last time we touched each other; there was something about the force that went through me! I didn't understand, but I extended my hand to him anyway, and he helped me out of the car. We walked up the steps while holding hands, and then he helped me to the porch. It was huge! It was filled with tropical plants, several swings, and six rocking chairs. The thing I liked the most was that it was screened all the way around. I have always loved wrap-around screened porches. The house looked like something I would have built for myself if I had the money to do so. We stopped at the door, and he took the key out of his pocket to unlock it.

"You go in first," he said, so I did.

The house was so bright; I looked around. It was beautiful! Everything was in its place, nothing like my place.

"Have a seat, and I'll be right back," he said.

I sat on an oversized white couch he had led me to; it felt soft and comfortable. It must have cost a small fortune. The other furniture was just as beautiful. He returned with a glass of what looked to be wine and handed it to me. I took it and said, "Thank you."

"You're welcome. Dinner will be ready soon. I hope you're hungry," he replied.

Yes, I am, I told him.

He smiled and returned to the kitchen.

While he was in the back, I decided to explore the area more. Not wanting him to see me, I kept a constant watch, keeping my ears open for any sound of his return. The house was immaculate! I'd never been in a home so clean and orderly. My mind started to wander: why did he need such a big house? It was just him, with no wife or children. How could he afford it? I didn't get to ask him what he did for a living last night, but he must be involved in something that pays well.

I heard him coming, I ran back to the couch and sat down, as if I had never moved.

"Did you enjoy your tour?" he asked.

How did he know? Feeling like I had just been caught, I smiled and said, "I hope you don't mind. I couldn't help but look around. Your home is so beautiful, and you must be very proud."

He didn't seem too excited.

Looking around, he said, "It's ok; I've had and seen better, much better," he repeated. The house smelled amazing! Whatever he was cooking made me wish he were finished. Wouldn't you know it, he cooks too! He is too good to be true! This is going to be a fantastic night. I had never had a guy cook for me before, and I knew he was a great cook from the smell of the food alone. He walked back to the kitchen while I sat there and behaved myself. Soon, he was back, letting me know dinner was ready to be served. He came over, took my hand, and escorted me to the dining room.

Entering the room took my breath away; it was candlelit, the table was adorned with fresh flowers, the China was exquisite, and the salad looked stunning. I couldn't wait to sink my teeth into it, considering I hadn't eaten all day. He asked again if I liked the house; my heart stopped once more. How did he know I was up looking around? I could not hear myself moving around, but he knew. He pulled out my chair, and I sat down. He then pushed my chair to the table, placing my salad plate in front of me. Then he said, "I hope you like Italian food. We have an Arugula and Parmesan salad to start us off." Walking to the other side of the table, he sat down and picked up his fork. I waited for him to offer to say grace, which he never did. I didn't attend church, but I always thanked God for my food. I bowed my head and said a quick thank you to God, then picked up my fork and took a bite of the salad.

"You've outdone yourself," I said. He looked at me and smiled; something about his smile caused me to lose it every time he did it. It seemed I couldn't control how I felt inside. When he smiles at me, something takes over. What is it? What is it about him that does that to me? It's not like he's trying to make me feel this way; as far as I can tell, he's being respectful and kind. I think it's me. Stop daydreaming, girl, and eat your salad. Everything will be fine if you just be you, I told myself. The salad looked and tasted great. We talked as we ate our first course. He told me about his travels around the world and the people he had met. People are his favorite. He loves dealing with them. "They're very easy to figure out," he said.

After talking for a while, he asked if I was finished with my salad, and I answered yes. Aiden took our plates into the kitchen. Shortly, he returned with the second course, Fettuccine Primavera. It smelled delicious, and the presentation was that of a five-star restaurant. He placed my plate in front of me, and with his food in his other hand, he walked over to the other side and sat down. Everything was going well. I took a bite, and he asked if I liked it. After a big sigh, I said, "It's delicious." Then I asked him if he was from an Italian family and where he'd learned to cook like this. He said he was not, and guessed it came naturally to him. "I wish it would come naturally to me," I replied, then asked how long he'd been cooking. I wanted to know if he could cook any food other than Italian.

"It doesn't matter what type of dish or what culture it's from. If it's food, I can cook it. Maybe I'll get the chance to show you if you agree to have dinner with me again tomorrow night," he said.

"I would love to. It would be nice to have this natural skill that you have. I wish I had the talent. Cooking is not something I'm good at, but I do my best. A girl must eat, right? Tomorrow night is a date," I said.

He looked at me and smiled again; this time, his smile looked a little strange. For a quick moment, I thought my eyes were playing tricks on me again. I closed my eyes and reopened them quickly. Looking at him, everything looked normal again. I took another bite of fettuccine. It was the best I'd ever eaten. My mind was playing tricks, and I knew it; nevertheless, I finished my dish.

"You are a fantastic chef," I told him.

"I have never considered myself a chef, but I guess you can say I am, among other things."

"You sure are! And you're the best one I know."

He thanked me, then said it was time for dessert. He took my plate and returned to the kitchen. I was full! My stomach was about to pop. How could I put anything else in it? Then he came out with two plates of the most beautiful pears. They stood upright on the plate. They were beautiful.

"Oh, my goodness, what do we have here?" I asked.

"Pear Al Vino Bianco," he replied.

"Pear Al what?" I asked.

"Pear Al Vino Bianco," he repeated.

"Aiden, they look gorgeous, and I can't wait to taste them."

He set the pear in front of me. I could smell the sweetness of the pear, with a hint of lemon and vanilla; it was unbelievable.

"I hope you like it," he said.

"I'm sure I will. I've enjoyed everything you've cooked, and I don't see this being any different."

I took a bite; it melted in my mouth.

"Is there lemon and vanilla in this?" I asked.

"Good girl, you figured it out. I love that you can figure things out," he said.

That was the second time he'd said that to me. Why did he keep saying that? I thought about him saying he loved figuring people out. Maybe this was his occupation: figuring people out. Perhaps he was a therapist or someone in a similar profession, or maybe he was a chef.

"What do you do for a living?" I asked.

"What do I do for a living?" he replied.

"Yes, what line of work are you in?"

For a quick second, he seemed to be shocked.

"I'm into all types of work."

"What does that mean?" I asked.

"It means I can do almost everything, and anything I can imagine, and want to do."

"Where do you work?" I asked again.

"I have several jobs, but my primary role is in the hospital's Psychiatric Unit."

That explains it! That is why you love figuring people out; it's your job! Now it all makes sense to me. I wondered why you kept saying it's good to know how to figure things out, and now I understand. I finished the pear.

"You prepared a fantastic meal, and you are an excellent cook. I can't wait until tomorrow night to do it again."

He smiled and said, "I was hoping to impress you tonight."

"Impress me? That's an understatement. I am more than impressed. This meal was out of this world."

"What would you like me to cook tomorrow night?" he asked.

"Wow! I don't know. Surprise me again. I'm sure I'll love whatever it is."

I laid back in my chair.

"Are you okay?" he asked.

"I'm great! Full as a tick on a dog, as my grandma used to say."

He laughed and stood up.

"Let me take your plate," he said.

"Sure. Can I help with the dishes?"

"No, but you're welcome to come in and keep me company if you'd like."

"I'd love to," I replied.

He pulled out my chair, and we walked into the kitchen together. It was large, and everything was in its place. Where were all the dishes from the first two courses? I did not hear him washing any of them. Besides, he came back too quickly with each course to have had time to wash them, but that doesn't mean he didn't. Every pot and pan was clean and hanging in its proper place. He's fast and neat, and I could see why he needed no help. He has it all under control, I thought to myself.

He has a very nice kitchen, and it was extremely well-organized.

"Everything is so organized and clean," I told him.

"Yes. I need things to be in order. How else will you get a job done if you're all over the place?" he replied.

Then he said that a person without organizational skills would not get far in this life or the next. I didn't respond to his comment; I was busy thinking of my disorganized house and how I could never let him in until it was in better condition than it was now. Thinking of his house again, I wondered if I would ever reach a point in my life where I could afford anything close to his place.

Then he asked me the magic question.

"So, what do you do for a living?"

I was ashamed, but I told him I was a travel agent anyway. I'd never been ashamed to tell anyone what I did for a living, and now, I was embarrassed—seeing what he had made me feel belittled and poor. I was poor, and I knew this, but this place made me feel things I never thought I would. I had always been ok with who I was and what I had, until now.

"Do you like your job?" he asked.

"I did love it until recently. I'm always sending people to places I can only dream about, and the pay sucks! I'm on a tight budget, trying to keep my head above water," I replied.

"Well, we will have to do something about that," he said.

I looked at him and smiled. It would be nice if it were to happen.

Finishing the dessert plates, he said, "I hope you enjoyed tonight."

"I thoroughly enjoyed it. It was terrific!" I told him.

"Let's get you home. It's late, and I know you have to work tomorrow. A little rest won't hurt you."

I looked at my watch, and it was late. It amazed me how time flew when I was with him. It was as if I had no sense of time. It was just Aiden and me; nothing else existed when I was in his presence.

"Is it ok if we have dinner again here at my place tomorrow night?" he asked. "If so, afterward, I would like to take you to the park."

What in God's name would we do in the park so late at night? It gets really dark out there. But why should I care? I'll be with him, I thought to myself. He put everything in its place. We walked into the living room, and he helped me with my coat.

"Thank you for everything. I enjoyed tonight. You are amazing," I said.

"I'm so glad you enjoyed yourself. Now let's get you home."

Walking to the car, I tripped, and he caught me.

"Thanks, Aiden. You have fast reflexes."

He smiled and opened my door, and I got in. He buckled me safely in, then went around, got in himself, and started the car. It didn't take long, and I was in front of my tiny house. He came around and opened my door. I got out, and he walked me to the door.

"Let me help you with that," he said.

I gave him my keys, and he unlocked the door and returned them to me. He pushed it open and said goodnight. I stood there and waited for a kiss, but it didn't happen. He hugged me and said goodnight again. I said goodnight, and he walked back to his car, waved, got in, and drove off. I walked in feeling like I was on cloud nine. Tonight was the best night of my life, I thought to myself. I got ready for bed and fell asleep with Aiden on my mind.

Day Three

I didn't sleep well that night; I had a terrifying dream. I dreamed I was walking in a big, open field, a beautiful field. The grass was lush and green, and the trees were massive and attractive. There were flowers I'd never seen before, many different colors. There were also animals, big and small, roaming out in the open field. I walked for a long time until I came across a part of the field that had no trees, no flowers, but the animals were still roaming around. I looked around to see if I could spot any trees in the area where I had walked. There were none.

I continued to walk, and before I knew it, I had walked much farther than I realized. The sun was so bright, the birds were singing, and I didn't have a care in the world.

As I walked a little farther, I started to feel like something or someone was following me. Suddenly, my mood changed, and I began to feel afraid. I stopped and turned around to see if anything or anyone was following. Then I saw it: a short distance behind me was a huge lion! He seemed to be on a rampage, attacking all the animals he could catch. The animals were scattered all over the field, running for their lives. The strange thing was that the animals made no sound as he attacked. I turned to look for a tree to climb, but there were none in sight. I stood there, hoping he wouldn't notice me. I don't know what made me think he wouldn't see me in the open field with no place to hide, and sure enough, it didn't take long for him to spot me standing there. He immediately started to run toward me at full speed. I turned to run, but it was pointless.

Before I could think, he attacked me from behind, knocking me to the ground! He then began biting the back of my neck. I yelled for help, but there was none; I was alone, getting eaten alive by this powerful beast. I tried to cover my head and neck, but it was too late. I felt the blood running down my back. The pain was unbearable! The more I fought, the more aggressive he became. Then I woke up. My heart was beating hard and fast, and it took me a minute to realize it was just a dream. I was still holding my head and crying. I sat there on the bed, shaking like a leaf in the wind, too upset to move right away. I sat there trying to compose myself.

After an hour or so, I finally pulled myself together and stood up. My knees were weak as if I had walked for hours. My neck hurt, and I felt a sense of fear inside. Even though I knew it was just a dream, my mind began thinking of Aiden and the night before. There was something I couldn't understand. His eyes troubled me, and I was never sure of what I saw when I was with him. I hated to think something was wrong; he was the man of my dreams, but something always felt off before or after seeing him. We always enjoyed each other's company, but the feeling remained. Not wanting to think about it any longer, I thought about breakfast. Come to think of it, I had not eaten breakfast in days. I'd been so busy working and preparing for my dates with Aiden that I'd entirely forgotten about eating in the mornings.

Looking in the fridge, I realized I had forgotten to go grocery shopping again. There was only out-of-date milk, a couple of eggs, and three bottles of water. There was nothing to eat. I decided to take thirty minutes before work to pick up some things from the store. This had to be a quick trip, as I only had a few minutes to spare. Going back upstairs, I moved quickly to beat the crowds. Running back down, I locked the door and jumped in the car. I wished I had the money to buy enough groceries to last more than a day. I hate grocery shopping;

it's a lot of work. First, you must make a list, which I'd forgotten to do! Then you have to go to the store, get what's on the list, put it in the cart, take it to the register, take it out of the cart, put it up on the conveyor belt, put it back in the cart, then put it in the car, take it out of the car, carry it into the house, unpack it, put it up, and if you want to eat, you have to cook it! It's just too much work for me. I hate it.

Arriving at the store, I took a look around the parking lot. There were many cars. I guess everyone else had the same idea. Just get in there and get it done, I told myself. I grabbed a cart and hurried in. Rushing down the aisles, I picked up the milk, eggs, bread, butter, fruit, vegetables, and a few other essentials I needed.

I wish I hadn't forgotten that list. I was sure I was forgetting something. Not paying attention, I bumped into someone else's cart. Looking up, I saw it was Liz!

"Liz, how are you?" I asked.

"Fine, stranger, how are you?" she replied.

"I'm great," I said.

She asked where I'd been the last couple of days. "I haven't seen or heard from you in days. I've called and left messages, but never heard anything back from you. I went by your house last night, but you weren't home."

"I'm sorry, Liz. I've been so busy with work and Aiden; I haven't had time for anything else. I'm in the store now because my fridge is empty. I didn't realize I had nothing to eat at home. Aiden's been cooking dinner for me the last two nights, which has been wonderful. I must say he's an excellent cook."

"Oh? What has he cooked for you?" she asked.

"He's cooked Italian, just like that, in a five-star restaurant, or better. His food is fantastic, and so is he." I told her we were having dinner again tonight.

"You two must have hit it off well to spend so much time together. Alex, I miss seeing you and talking to you," she said.

I looked at her and smiled. I promised her we would see each other soon. I wanted to tell her all about him and what I had seen in his eyes, but honestly, I wasn't sure what I had seen. I didn't want her to think I was crazy, so I kept it to myself.

Liz and I have been friends our entire lives. We grew up together. Our parents were best friends, and so are we. We attended the same church regularly when we were younger and always shared everything with each other. Liz still attends church regularly. She always invites me to go, but I haven't. After my breakup with Jacob, I haven't wanted to return to church, not because Jacob attends with his new wife, but because I didn't understand why God allowed things to go the way they did, so I stopped going altogether.

I still think about church and God, but I don't go. Liz often reminds me that I shouldn't blame God for what happened. Sometimes, I guess I do blame him, but deep inside, I know God delivered me from a terrible relationship, and I'm happy about that. Sometimes, I wish he had changed things in my favor. I loved Jacob, but that's water under the bridge now. I have Aiden, and I think I'm falling in love with him.

Liz called my name, and I realized I had been daydreaming again.

"Sorry about that, Liz. My mind seems to wander nowadays."

"It's okay. I miss seeing you. When can we get together again?" she asked.

"I have dinner with Aiden again tonight. After dinner, he's taking me to the park."

"The park?" she repeated. "Is something going on in the park tonight?"

I replied that I could think of nothing, but Aiden had something planned, and I was excited to see what it was.

"It sounds like you are having fun."

"I am, and I hope it lasts forever!"

"Wow, you're feeling him," she said.

"Liz, I cannot tell you how happy I've been over the last two days. He makes me feel like a queen, focuses on me, and makes me feel special."

"I wish you both love and luck," she replied.

"Thank you, Liz. I must go now. I will call you later."

I rushed to pay for the groceries, put them in the car, and returned home. Grabbing the bags, I dashed inside, putting the groceries away as quickly as possible, and ran upstairs to prepare for work, hoping the day would be good. Thank God my job is right around the corner.

I had just clocked in when the phone rang, my first customer of the day, with a request to schedule a trip for two to New South Wales.

"It's our **Thirty-first** anniversary," the man stated on the other end. "This is a surprise trip for her. She will love it," he said.

I agreed and scheduled their trip and began to think about how nice it would be to take a journey with Aiden. I would get a discount if we ever did. Smiling, I answered another phone call. This time, it was a daughter calling to schedule a trip for her single mother.

"I want to plan a wonderful trip for my mother. She has always been fond of the Caribbean," she said. "I would love it if you could help me pick a special place for her to enjoy herself."

"Okay, let's see what we can find. What about St. Kitts and Nevis?" I asked. "St. Kitts will be perfect for your mom. It has shores of soft sand, a lively nightlife if that's her thing, and delicious food. She can also take a trip over to Nevis if she wants quiet and relaxation from the wild side," I told her.

"That sounds lovely. I think she'll love it. Let's book it," she replied.

After booking her, the phone rang again. I was on a roll, I thought.

What a busy morning! It usually takes an hour or two between calls, but today it was back-to-back. This is good. It doesn't give me time to think about my personal life, and it makes the time pass quickly. Let's keep it moving. The faster the time goes, the faster I can see Aiden, I told myself.

The day passed quickly.

On the way home, Aiden called me to remind me of our date later that night; how could I forget it?

"So, seven it is?" he asked.

"Yes, seven it is," I replied.

"Great, I'll see you tonight," he said and hung up.

Then I realized I had forgotten to pick up something to wear out tonight. Oh, my goodness! This is not good; the day was great, and now it could be a disaster. I'd had to shop for the last two dates, and now I had nothing new to impress him. Lacking the money or time to shop, I needed to find something nice in my closet that wasn't from so many years ago. Looking through my closet, I found a pair of pants and a shirt to match. I told myself they would have to do for now, and it wasn't too bad; this would tell me if he liked me or my clothes. Again, I had to shower quickly and iron my hair flat to be on time. This was beginning to be too much; I had forgotten how exhausting this dating life could be. I didn't have time to breathe, but it was worth it every time I saw him.

It was seven sharp, and the doorbell rang! It couldn't be seven already; I hadn't even put my pants on. Rushing, I yelled out, "Just a minute!" I put my pants on and ran downstairs to open the door.

"You look lovely," he said.

"Thank you. How are you tonight?" I asked.

"I'm great. Are you ready?" he replied.

"Yes," I answered.

"Let's go," he said.

He helped me down the steps to his car and opened the door; I felt like a princess entering my carriage. He always made me feel so special, and I loved it. I really believe I'm falling for him. It's only been two days, but I feel like I've known him for a lifetime.

We arrived at his house, and he helped me out of the car and up to the porch. Then, we walked up to the door, which he opened, allowing me to step inside. Again, I was amazed at how big and clean it was.

"Have a seat, but first give me your coat," he said.

"Sure," I answered.

I gave him my coat and sat down.

"Can I bring you a drink or something else?" he asked.

Thinking about the last time he asked, and I said no, this time, I said, "Yes, please bring me something to drink."

"Sure, I'll be back in a second," he replied.

He left the room and returned with a wine glass with a pineapple on the side.

"What's in there?" I asked.

"Oh, just a little Pineapple, Orange, and Mint Punch."

He handed me the glass, and I took a sip and licked my lips.

"What do you think?" he asked.

"It's delicious; I could drink this all night!" I replied.

"There's more when you want it," he said and walked away.

Before I finished my drink, he came to collect me for dinner.

"The first course is served," he said.

"I'm ready," I replied.

He reached for my hand. I thought of the last time we held hands; it was magical. I placed my hand in his. Again, I felt that same feeling coming over me; my body felt limp.

"Let's go to the dining room table," he said, and we went in.

The table was beautiful, and the dishes were very colorful and different from any I'd ever seen. I walked over to the table, and he pulled out my chair; I sat down. On the table was a very colorful fruit salad; the colors were bright and fresh. It consisted of chopped oranges, pineapples, kiwi, and raspberries, with a few mint leaves for garnish. The salad also had a transparent orange dressing on top. He sat down, and we began to eat. Stopping, I repeated a quick prayer. The fruit salad was excellent.

"How did he come up with these dishes?" I asked myself.

I began to wonder if I could live off this food and decided I could; it didn't take me long to finish my salad. Looking over at him, he wasn't far behind me.

He asked, "How was your day? Did you get any rest before dinner?"

"Not really. Today was a busy day; work was also busy. I scheduled many vacations today, went to the grocery store earlier this morning before work, then before I knew it, the doorbell rang, and it was   you."
He smiled and said, "I hope you're not too tired to go to the park tonight."

"Are you kidding me? I'm not tired, I'm looking forward to it!"

"Great, I have something special planned for you."

He finished his salad and asked for my plate, which he then took into the kitchen.

Again, I didn't hear any water running; he came back with the second course, which made my mouth water. Putting my plate in front of me, he walked to the other end of the table and sat down. He placed his plate on the table. I looked over at him, and he said, "We have orange chicken with a hint of orange-flavored mash, orange-glazed carrots, and an excellent piece of Artisan bread if you'd like some. Dig in."

I didn't even know you could put oranges in mashed potatoes, but when I tasted them, they were awesome! The potatoes were delicious; I'd never had this flavor before, but the hint of orange was on point.

"Where did you learn this recipe?" I asked.

"It's something I threw together." He replied.

He couldn't have just thrown this together. Maybe he didn't want me to know his secrets. The orange chicken and carrots were terrific, too. I thought about the third course and how I would finish it, and then he said there was none. I was relieved; my stomach was full. He hadn't skimped on the food.

"Would you like more to drink?" he asked.

"No, thank you. I'm full."

"Great, maybe we should head to the park before it gets too late."

We put on our coats, and he escorted me to the car. He opened my door and helped me inside. I wondered what we would do at the park this late at night, but it didn't matter; I didn't mind. He got in the car, and we headed over; it was very dark when we arrived. I'm usually inside when night comes, but this was a change for me; everything looked different in the dark. I didn't even recognize the place where we parked.

"It's dark out here," I said.

"Yes, it is," he replied, "but I am here with you, and I'll take good care of you."

He opened his door, got out, walked around, and helped me out of the car. Taking my hand, he told me to turn around and close my eyes. I did, and he tied a cloth over them.

"No peeking, this is a special surprise," he said.

"Okay, just don't let me bump into anything."

"I got you," he replied.

Then he led me away from the car. I didn't know where he was taking me, but I trusted him somehow; I knew I was safe with him. We walked for a few minutes, and then he stopped.

"We're here now. Take three steps up."

I took three steps up, and he led me to a table. He turned my body around and told me I could sit. I couldn't see a thing, but I sat down, trusting there was a seat behind me. After I sat, he took the blindfold off, and I was surprised at what I saw.

We were sitting in a small gazebo surrounded by lights and flowers. The place was beautiful and well-decorated. A live band sat in front of me. They began to play soft music, and then he sat next to me.

Alex, "Do you like the surprise?" He asked.

"Yes! This was more than I expected, and I love it!"

It was special. I looked around, and on another decorated table was a large platter of chocolate-dipped strawberries, several different kinds of cheese, and fresh fruit. My eyes began to well up with tears.

He asked if anything was wrong?"

I replied, "Nothing was wrong. Everything was wonderful and couldn't get any better."

He turned to me and reached for my hand again. I happily gave it to him. Helping me stand, he pulled me closer to him and put his arms around me. I placed my arms around his waist. I didn't know what to think. This was too much; I must be dreaming. This guy was unbelievable. Tightening my arms around him, I closed my eyes and laid my head on his chest. He held me close, and we stood still for a while. My heart was overjoyed; words couldn't express my joy. Aiden and I felt a strong chemistry between us. I could tell by how he held me and touched the small of my back. The music was magical, evoking emotions I had never felt before, and I am sure that Aiden also played a significant role in it.

He said, "I am here with you; I'll take care of you."

I knew I could trust him, and I knew he was someone I wanted to spend the rest of my life with. Even though it had only been three days, I somehow just felt it.

"He has to be the one for me," I told myself.

How I wish this night would last forever. I didn't feel the cold or mind the dark. Aiden had won me over, and I hoped he knew it. We danced the night away with him holding me close, and then he whispered, "I'd better get you home; it's late, and we must get some rest."

My mind was very far away. I was in heaven and didn't want to come back to earth, but I knew he was right, so I agreed. He held me close for a few more minutes and then let me go when the music stopped. He walked over to the table and instructed the waiter to box up the strawberries, cheese, and fruit. The waiter bent down behind the table, picked up the most exquisite, transparent glass-like box, and then put all the food inside. I marveled at the box; again, it was so beautiful.

"Where did you find that box?" I asked.

He said, "I didn't find it; I made it, especially for you. It's something you can keep forever."

My mouth dropped open; I didn't know what to say, but it was beautiful! "And thank you."

He smiled and said it was not a problem. Then he placed his hand on the small of my back, as if to say, "Let's go."

Walking to the car, I thought of the three nights I'd spent with him, but tonight was just unbelievable. We had been as close to each other as we'd ever been, and it felt great. He opened my door, and I got in. On the drive home, he was quiet.

Then he said, "What about tomorrow?"

"Whatever you want," I answered.

"What about eight tomorrow night?"

"Sure, I'd love to."

We talked briefly, and before I knew it, I was home again. He walked me to the door, and I gave him the key; he then unlocked it. Standing there, I waited for him to kiss me goodnight. Surely tonight must be the night after all that happened. I knew he would kiss me, but instead of a kiss, I received another hug and goodnight. Then he turned, walked to his car, and drove off again.

Maybe he doesn't believe in kissing before marriage, I thought. I walked inside and placed my beautiful box in the refrigerator, then went upstairs and got ready for bed. As I lay there, I thought about how our night had gone. Everything was terrific, and I wanted more of everything I had experienced the last three nights. I wasn't sure about it, but it was going great. I asked God not to let it change, and I have talked to God more often lately than ever. I wanted God to keep him in my life. Lying there, I waited for the bad gut feeling I would get now and then, but tonight, nothing! Nothing at all. I felt great!

Perhaps God had heard my prayers. Now my purpose was to win him over to like me as much as I liked him. I lay there on my bed, wondering what my life would be like if I could see him daily for the rest of my life. Would it be as good as I thought, or would it be a disaster? I didn't know, but I was willing to find out. I couldn't see it any other way, but for now, it was terrific. He was a wonderful guy, and I felt he was the one for me. I was happier tonight than I had been in years, and it was all because of Aiden. I said a quick prayer, asking God to keep him in my life, and then I drifted off to sleep.

Day Four

Early the next morning, I woke up feeling great; I called Liz to see if she could take a day off so we could spend it together. She said she would. I called my job and asked for the day off to spend with my best friend, whom I'd not seen or spoken to since I met Aiden, except briefly in the grocery store. We met up around ten a.m., and it was great to see her again; I'd missed her, and I'm sure she missed me, too.

We planned nothing; we would do whatever we wanted today. We met in a parking lot halfway between her house and mine. I jumped into the car with her to grab brunch. We sat and talked for a couple of hours at the restaurant, catching up on each other's lives. She told me how demanding work had become, how tired she was, and how she hadn't had a chance to do anything she wanted to do because her life was so busy. I felt so bad; I'd been so focused on my own life with my job and Aiden that I hadn't even thought about Liz or anything else. She smiled and told me that sharing food at the same table with me was something she enjoyed. I reached for her hand, held it for a minute, and told her how wonderful it was to get together again; it was a great morning. Liz and I were together, and we were having a wonderful time. Afterward, we decided we would see a movie, relax, and enjoy ourselves. I wanted to tell her everything about Aiden.

After giving it considerable thought, I decided I would discuss it with her. "Liz, I want to tell you about Aiden; as you know, we've been seeing a lot of each other lately since we met, and I feel like he's the one. I've been asking God to let this work out."

She looked at me and smiled, then asked, "Have you been praying? If so, that's great. I thought you had almost given up on God. What made you start praying again?"

"Well, things have been going so well with Aiden, and I want it to last. God can help with that if He wants that relationship for me. Don't you agree?" I asked.

"Wow! What if He chooses it's not His will? Then what?" she asked.

"I never thought it wouldn't be His will. It's such a wonderful relationship, and I couldn't see Him not wanting it to last. Why would He not?" I asked. "Doesn't He want me to be happy?"

"I'm not saying He doesn't. I'm just asking if you continue to pray, and He disagrees with your request and doesn't work in your favor, then what?"

"Liz, I have never forgotten God. Even though I don't attend church, I know God is real. I regret having stopped going to church, but I've done it for so long that it now seems normal to me. I believe that God is always with me and loves me. I need to find my way back to Him. I have prayed and asked Him for this one thing."

"Alex, you know God hasn't left you; you need to choose to come back to Him. He's waiting with open arms to receive you back. You know this. You should start coming to church with me again," she said.

"When I get a chance, I will," I replied. "Now, let me tell you about Aiden. I have never met anyone like him. He's hard to figure out."

I don't understand anything about him, but he seems like the perfect guy. I wanted to share with her the feeling I got when he held my hand and the quick changes I saw in his eyes, but I didn't want her to think badly of him, so I only told her things I thought she would believe and be okay with.

Knowing Liz for as long as I have, I knew she would not judge me, but I didn't know what I felt or saw, so I didn't say anything about those things. I also wanted to share my gut feelings with her, but again, I only wanted to convey positive aspects of the relationship. My gut told me to tell her, but my mind said not to. I kept quiet about those three things; I didn't want Aiden to be perceived as a strange person. We talked until about noon, and then we headed to the movies. Unsure of what we would see, we decided to pick a movie upon arrival. The parking lot was empty; it was the middle of the day, and most people were at work. We were happy it wasn't crowded, because we dealt with people all day long at our jobs, so it was nice not having many people around. We went inside and decided to watch *A Cinderella Story*; it was a great movie. I compared it to my relationship with Aiden. They were so in love, and so was I, I thought. Liz and I both enjoyed it.

After the movie, we went to get yogurt. Our day together was great; we were like we were before Aiden came into the picture.

Liz asked when I would see Aiden again. I told her we had another date later tonight, and that's why I wanted to see her today. I've been swamped over the last few days, and I just wanted to spend some time with her.

"I've missed you; we must make time for each other," I told her.

She agreed that we would get together again real soon.

We finished our yogurt and hugged each other.

"I suppose I'd better get home; I have a lot to do before Aiden picks me up tonight."

"I hope it all works out for you both. You seem happy since you've started seeing him, and I'm thrilled," she said.

44

"You know, Liz, sometimes it scares me."

"Why does it scare you? And how so?"

"I don't know for sure. It's hard to explain; it's almost too good to be true."

"Are you sure you're okay?" she asked.

"Yes, I'm sure everything is fine."

Liz took me back to my car, and we said our goodbyes. It was lovely spending most of the morning and afternoon with her. We have always enjoyed each other's company. She is my best friend, and I miss and love her. She's the sister I never had. No matter what happens with Aiden, Liz and I will always be best friends.

I was happy to get home. We had a busy day, and even though we did nothing but chill, we still had a great time. Many things had to be done before tonight. What would it be like tonight, I wondered. It couldn't get any better than last night. Last night was the best night of all the nights we've spent together. We got as close to each other as we had ever been, and it was an incredible feeling being in his arms.

I didn't know what he could do tonight to outdo last night. I hurried inside and sat down for a quick minute. After taking a deep breath, I thought of what I would wear.

Oh, my goodness! This dating thing was stressful, and I always wanted to look my best for him, but I was running out of clothes and couldn't afford to buy new ones. I'll have to choose something out of my closet again, I thought.

Jumping up, I ran upstairs to get something nice to wear. I picked a pair of black and white polka-dot pants and a long, black, flared-sleeve shirt.

"This should go well together," I thought.

Then I got into the shower and washed my hair. I stood there for a while, not realizing how tired I was until that hot water ran over my aching body. Wanting to stay in longer, I forced myself to get out. I looked over at the clock. I only had an hour and a half remaining before he arrived.

"Wow, how time flies," I told myself, pulling out the blow dryer. No time for waving, curling, or pinups, just straight ironing again. This was my new look. I only have time for a flat iron, nothing else, and if I get that done, I will be doing well. An hour and fifteen minutes passed, and I felt worn out.

"God, just let me make it through tonight," I asked.

And then it happened; all of a sudden, my stomach felt like it was tied in knots. I bent over to see if that would help. It hadn't happened to me lately. I couldn't understand this. It only started when I was with Aiden, or after I'd been with him. Come to think of it, it started when I first met him. It had to be a coincidence, but I've never felt like this as far as I can remember. I wished it would go away, and in a few minutes, it did.

I finished getting ready and sat down. I felt a bit queasy.

"Not now; he will be here shortly. Stop with the foolishness, girl," I told myself.

The doorbell rang, and I got up to answer it. There he stood with flowers again.

"These are for you," he said.

"How beautiful! Let me put them in water. Come in."

This was the first time I had invited him into my place. I had found a little time to pick up things. As I walked away, I could feel his eyes wandering around.

"Nice little place you have here."

"It's okay. Nothing on the scale of yours, for sure."

"Are you ready?" I asked.

"If you are," he replied.

We got in the car and drove off. This time, we headed in a different direction.

"You didn't cook tonight?" I asked.

"No, not tonight. I thought we would go out to dinner, if that's okay with you."

"Sure. I was wondering if you were going to cook every time we had dinner. All that gourmet cooking must wear you out."

"Not really, just thought you may want a change."

"Aiden, your cooking is divine. I love it and could eat it every day."

"That's nice," he replied, but tonight let's try someone else's food. How about a nice juicy steak?" he asked.

"Steak? I love steak. A baked potato with butter and sour cream and a side salad is one of my favorite meals."

"Good, then you should love the steakhouse we're going to," he said. "I've heard good things about it."

We drove for about forty-five minutes and arrived at the beautiful Chiltepin Steakhouse restaurant. It's named after a spicy pepper, and they're known for cooking with spice. Some people say the steaks are to die for," he said.

"I hope I can get one that's not too spicy. I want to enjoy it; I can't take the heat if it's too hot," I told him.

"I'm sure they have mild spices you can enjoy," he replied.

We got out of the car and went in. The aroma was to die for, smelling like heaven on earth. My mouth started watering from the smell alone, and I was salivating before I sat down.

"Wow! If they tasted anything like they smelled, I was in for a treat. It could be the best steak I've ever eaten."

We were seated and given a menu. Kobe Filets, Japanese Beef, Prime Rib Roast, Premium Angus, and many more were on the list, and they were not cheap.

Looking at the price, I thought he might change his mind and tell me we needed to leave, but instead, he looked over at me and said, "Pick anything you want."

I felt like a sponge, sucking up his hard-earned money.

"Are you sure? We can go somewhere else if we need to."

He looked at me, and I saw something in his eyes that caused me to take a double-take.

What was wrong with me? I must be going crazy. If it's not my stomach, it's my eyes, I thought.

"Is something wrong?" he asked.

"No, I just got something in my eyes. Must be the smoke off the peppers," I replied.

I tried not to stare at him. What in God's name is going on? I thought. I only seem to have this happen to me when I'm with him. Any other time, I seem to be fine. I think I'm losing my mind. I must be so excited about this relationship that I'm losing it, I thought.

"Do you see anything you like?" he asked.

That reminded me of the first night we met. Liz asked me the same question when she caught me staring at him. Looking at my menu again, I decided to have the trimmed American-style Kobe filet mignon with the Tam jalapeño peppers, which seemed to be the mildest pepper I could find on the menu. He ordered a Japanese rib-eye steak, the fourteen-ounce one. That one alone cost around $150 or more. We ordered baked potatoes and a side salad to accompany our expensive steaks.

That meal would have cost me a week and a half's pay. I had hit a goldmine. He was young and well-off. I wondered where he got all of his money from. It couldn't be from the hospital. I'm around his age, and nothing like this was happening to me. I want what he has, I thought.

After a short time, our meal was placed in front of us. The smell was amazing, and the steaks still had a little sizzle; the potatoes were huge and perfectly cooked, and the salad was fresh and full of color. They even brought a freshly baked loaf of sun-dried tomato bread with finely chopped mild Hatch green peppers.

The waiter cautioned Aiden to be careful. "You've chosen the Bhut Jolokia Chocolate pepper, and it's dangerously hot; please be careful," he said. Aiden smiled and moved his water over so that the waiter could put his plate down on the table.

"Thank you," he told the waiter.

"You're welcome," he replied, and then added, "Remember to be careful," before walking away.

It looked and smelled great. He took a bite, and I asked, "How's your steak? Is it too hot? Remember, the waiter said you must be careful with the pepper you ordered; it's dangerously hot!"

He looked at me, gave me one of those gorgeous smiles, and said, "It's not hot."

"Are you sure? Have you ever had it before?" I asked.

After insisting that he be careful, he agreed to do so. I looked down at my plate; there was no offer to say grace, so I said a quiet one for myself and cut into my steak.

As I cut it open, my mouth filled with water, just as it had when I first walked in. I put a small piece in my mouth, and it melted like ice; it was the most tender and delicious steak I had ever eaten.

"How is it?" Aiden asked.

"To die for, the best I've ever eaten. And the pepper is just right, not too hot. It's the perfect mildness."

"How about yours?" I asked.

"It's so good, and hot just the way I like it," he said with a smile.

"Is it too hot?" I asked.

"No, not at all," he replied.

By this time, the heat from his pepper began to make my eyes water, and I began to clear my throat.

"Are you okay?" he asked again.

"Yes, I'm just feeling the heat from your peppers. How can you eat that? It's so spicy."

"It's not bad. A little spice never hurt anybody," he said, as he put another piece in his mouth.

I watched as he chewed. I waited for him to choke or grab his water, but he did neither. He cut another piece and raked some of the peppers and sauce onto the steak, then put it in his mouth. Watching him eat made me nervous; those were dangerously hot, and he was eating them as if they were sweet peppers.

I couldn't eat while watching him; I didn't want him to choke. He noticed me watching him and asked if I was going to eat or if I wanted to watch him enjoy his meal. I rubbed my eyes and took another bite of mine. I must admit that my steak was excellent, as were the potatoes and the salad. Then I began to wonder why I hadn't heard of or seen this place before. I should have, considering Liz and I are always looking for new places to eat; no one in our small town must have known about this exquisite place.

It didn't take Aiden long to finish off his hot steak; it seemed not to affect him. He ate it as if it were a grilled steak with salt and pepper. His tongue must be made of iron. Maybe that's why he hasn't tried to kiss me yet. Having that thought enter my mind made me smile, and then I finished my excellent meal.

"Any dessert?" he asked.

"Do they have chocolate cake?" I replied.

"I don't know. Let's get the waiter over here and ask," he said.

He raised his finger in the air, and the waiter came over.

"Do you have any chocolate cake?" he asked.

"Sure. What would this place be without peppers and chocolate cake?"

Aiden told him, "We would like a slice of your best chocolate cake."

"Would you like the pepper glaze on it?" the waiter asked.

Aiden looked at me and asked if I would like the mild chocolate pepper sauce.

"My Lord! I've never had chocolate cake with chocolate pepper sauce, but if it were a mild sauce, I would try it. Please make sure it's mild," I asked.

"I will," the waiter said, and he walked away. Shortly after, he returned with the cake, which looked amazing.

He looked over at Aiden and said, "Sir, I see you survived the peppers. The last person who ate them ended up in an ambulance. You seem to have taken them quite well."

"It was nothing," Aiden replied.

"Enjoy your cake, ma'am," he said, and returned to the back of the restaurant.

I took a bite of the cake, and again, it was to die for; it was the best chocolate cake I'd ever eaten. I asked Aiden if he wanted a taste, and he said, "No, you enjoy it. Maybe next time."

I didn't know who the better cook was, Aiden or the chef at this restaurant. The chef here was terrific, but Aiden was better. I made the decision based on what I had eaten, which was cooked by each one.

We sat for a while longer after I finished my cake and talked. I thanked him for an excellent and expensive meal, to which he replied, "No problem."

I noticed that nothing seemed to excite him the way it did me; he seemed okay with whatever.

He looked at his watch. "You know, it's later than I thought," he said. "We have a forty-five-minute drive home, so we'd best be going now. Can you take a day off work tomorrow? I know it's tough on you right now, but I'll pay you triple your wages if you'd like. I want to take you on a special drive."

"Sure," I replied, thinking of how I could pull this off after taking yesterday off to be with Liz. But for triple pay, I would come up with something. "Just let me make a phone call when I get home, and I will let you know."

He smiled and said, "If you'd call me tonight to let me know, I'm sure I won't be asleep."

"What time is too late for me to call?" I asked.

"No time is too late; I'll be up."

"All right! I'll call you as soon as I get an answer from my supervisor."

"Let's go home now. We have a big day ahead of us tomorrow," he said.

We walked out and started the forty-five-minute drive home. I felt I would be tired on that drive he was taking me on tomorrow; I could hardly stay awake on the way home. I tried not to let it show.

We arrived at my house, and he parked the car and said, "Let's get you inside."

We walked up to the porch, and he opened my door as usual; I stood there waiting to see what he would do next.

"Did you enjoy yourself?" he asked.

"Yes. I had a fantastic night."

Before I finished speaking, he interrupted and asked if he could kiss me on the cheek.

I said, "Sure, you can!"

And sure enough, he did a kiss on the cheek.

He said goodnight, and I went inside.

"He's getting there," I thought. "Maybe tomorrow will be the day."

It didn't take me long to reach my boss; I told her that something important had come up and I needed to take another day off. She wasn't happy about it, but she gave it to me anyway.

I called Aiden to let him know we were set for tomorrow morning.

"Okay, I'll pick you up around 10 a.m. Get plenty of rest tonight."

"I'll certainly do so," I replied.

I was about to pass out from the food I'd eaten at the restaurant and the long drive home. I put on my pajamas and then set my alarm. I was too excited to sleep right away, so I just lay there for a while. All I could think about was Aiden and how happy I was with him.

After Jacob, I never thought I would feel this way again, but Aiden had changed all that. I felt good about myself, him, and our relationship. Now I just had to wait and see what would happen next.

Day Five

The following day, I woke up from a horrible dream; I dreamed I was out in my yard, working in my flower bed, picking up sticks and raking leaves that had fallen from the trees in the yard. In my dream, I had gotten up early to finish this task before leaving for work. All was going well until I stood up to carry some weeds around back to put on the burn pile. I looked down the street and saw a pack of dogs running straight toward me; I dropped the weeds and didn't know what to do next. I knew I had to get to safety, but was I to run? I've always heard it said that if you run from a dog, it will surely make it chase you. And I wasn't the fastest runner, but was I fast enough to reach the door and get inside to safety before they attacked me? The look on their faces said it all: they were mad, and they appeared to be focused on me.

As they got closer, I realized it was now or never; I could stand there and wait for them to attack, or I could take my chances and try to get inside before they reached me. I rushed for the door and barely made it inside. Immediately after shutting the door, I could hear them hitting against it. I quickly locked the door, turned my back to it, and slid down to the floor. My heart raced. I couldn't believe it! "Where did these dogs come from?" I asked myself. "Thank you, God, for letting me get safely inside the house." I continued to sit there, trying to gather my thoughts. I sat on the floor with my back against the door. I could hear them clawing at the door and barking. And just as suddenly as they came, they were gone; everything stopped. I wondered if they would start barking and clawing at the door again, but they never did.

About ten minutes passed, and I crawled to the window to look outside. I stayed low, lifting my head high enough to peek out of the window in case they were still out there. I looked as far to the left and the right as I could, and then I looked straight ahead as far as I could. There were no signs of them; it appeared they had left, but I was too afraid to open the door to go back outside, fearing they might still be out there somewhere. When I woke up, I wondered what it was all about. In my dreams lately, I'm constantly being attacked by something wild or deadly. I was shaken up a bit. Something was going on, and for the last four days, I had sensed that something was different, but I couldn't quite put my finger on it. I knew something I'd never been through was happening to me, and it was quite puzzling. I began to think more intensely about it.

I sat for a few minutes. I felt so sluggish; I was worn out from a lack of sleep and rest, and I had no time to think. Time was passing quicker than I could think. I decided my thoughts had to be put on the back burner; I only had a few hours to prepare for my date with Aiden. I only hoped he had not planned such a physically challenging day. "Please let it be simple," I thought. Slowly getting out of bed, I stretched to loosen up my bones. I was so stiff and sore that I thought a hot shower would help, so I quickly jumped in. It felt good, but I couldn't stay in for long; I had a lot to do. Aiden didn't say where we were going, and I didn't ask, but now I wish I had.

Not knowing how to dress, I picked something casual, hoping it would be ok. Wondering where he would take me next was always exciting. I finished dressing and put my hair up in a ponytail. If I were only going to take a country drive, a ponytail would be just fine. Anyway, I'd been cooking my hair flat-ironing it every night, and it needed a rest. Looking in the mirror, I didn't look too bad, not as good as I could have looked, but I was just too tired to do anything more to fix myself up.

Slowly, I walked down the stairs to the kitchen. "What can I find for breakfast?" I thought. I opened the fridge and took out yogurt and some fruit from the beautiful transparent box that Aiden had given me the night before. Looking at the box more closely, I wondered where he had gotten the materials to make such a unique and gorgeous piece. It was like nothing I'd ever seen and must have cost a fortune. I stared at it for a long time while holding it up to the light. It was breathtaking. "Liz must take a look at this; maybe she's seen something like it," I said to myself.

Liz had traveled more than I ever would. Maybe somewhere in her travels, she had encountered something similar. I'd never seen such a beautiful piece. After admiring the box for a while, I put it back in the fridge and sat down to eat the fruit I had taken out of it. I didn't have a chance to eat any of it the night he gave it to me. When I tasted it, all I could say was, "Wow!" Amazingly, the taste was quite different from what I was familiar with. "Where did he get the fruit?" I thought. Everything he gave me tasted significantly better than what I was accustomed to eating. If the taste remained this fresh and tasted this good a day or so later, think what it must have tasted like the other night when it was fresh. I couldn't stop eating it; it was delicious. Going back for more and saving some for later, I finished what I had taken out, then ate my yogurt. "That was the best breakfast I'd ever eaten," I thought. I licked my lips and went back upstairs. Sitting on my bed, I began to think about what today might bring, which made me smile.

The last four days had been like heaven. I'd met a man who was out of this world, so kind, loving, respectful, and the best chef you could ever have cook for you. What more could a girl ask for? I'd hit a goldmine. The only thing lacking was that he hadn't asked me to be his girl yet. Would he ever ask, or was this just a friend thing to him? I wanted more than that with him. I wanted a relationship—a possible husband. A family would be wonderful. Could it happen to me? I lay back on the bed, looking over at the clock. I only had twenty-three minutes, and my prince would be here to pick up his princess. Smiling, I closed my eyes and said a quick prayer for a good, fun, and stress-free day.

At 10 a.m., the doorbell rang. This guy was never late. I jumped up and looked in the mirror. I took the hair tie off my hair, rubbed my hair all to the back, put the tie back on, and ran downstairs to answer the door.

"Good morning, bright eyes," he said.

"Good morning to you," I replied.

For the first time since we'd been out, he wore a nice pair of dark sunglasses. He looked so handsome and cool.

"How was your night?" he asked.

"Good. I slept like a baby. What about you?"

"Great," he answered.

I was glad I hadn't dressed because he wore a pair of jeans and a T-shirt, which was a change. He always wore a suit. I wondered where we were going. He'd never picked me up dressed in jeans before.

"Thank you, God," I thought. "This must be a laid-back day," and I couldn't be happier.

"Are you ready to go?" he asked. "Maybe you should bring a sweater, even though it will be a warmer day today. The forecast calls for seventy-two degrees, quite different from yesterday, but you'd better grab one just in case they're wrong," he said.

I grabbed a sweater, and he reached for my hand. I placed my hand in his, and he held it tightly. I waited for a few seconds, and just like clockwork, there it was again. It felt like electricity had jolted me. Again, I pulled my hand back in shock.

"Is something wrong?" he asked.

"Oh no! Just a little shock."

Then he reached for my hand again. I extended my hand, and he helped me into his car.

Helping me inside, he said, "Today, we will relax."

Relax! Relaxation is what I prayed for! Thank you, God," I thought to myself. I was thrilled to hear the word "relax." I needed relaxation, and today, I would get some.

"I've packed up a picnic lunch for later. I hope you like picnics and being outside in nature," he said.

"I love picnics and nature. I can't get enough of it, considering I spend most of my time indoors. Today is well appreciated. Let's get going," I responded, smiling.

Then we drove off. We had great conversations as we traveled to our destination. When I asked where we were going, he wouldn't tell me. It was a surprise.

He would say, "Wait and see. You will love it."

It was true. I was sure I would love it, even though I didn't know where he was taking me. I trusted him completely. It was like he knew everything about me: the foods, the flowers, and everything else in my life seemed to be known to him. Maybe he's been talking to Liz or someone who knows me well. So far, I've loved everything he's planned. It's been all my favorite things.

After about three and a half hours, we pulled up to a beautiful, bronze-locked gate that had a sign on it that said, 'Private Property.' There appeared to be a garden of some sort beyond the gate. What is this place? And who lives here? I asked. I live here he said. Huh! I thought you lived in the house not far from me, I replied. I do, but I also own this place.

This guy was on a level I could never reach. He had two places to call home, and I could barely keep up with the rent on the small place where I live. I didn't know what to think. I must have missed something along the way. There must be more he has to tell me about his life and how he can afford all these wonderful things.

He parked the car, got out, unlocked the gate, then got back in and continued to drive along the long driveway. As we drove, the landscape was out of a Southern Living Magazine; it was full of gorgeous hedges that had been cut into different shapes and sizes. Some flowers were fully bloomed, displaying a wide range of colors. The grass was as green as it would be in midsummer. I looked around and saw a large pond with four fountains; they were shooting water up one after the other, accompanied by two yellow and two golden lights.

As the water gushed out, my eyes were fixed on the fountains, waiting for all four to complete their turn. It was like we had driven into paradise. He moved along the longest driveway I'd ever traveled on, and in the far back was a massive mansion with stained glass on every window. The house itself was made of a material I'd never seen before; it was a sight to behold. It had a huge wrap-around porch, complete with stairs, something I had always dreamed of.

My heart felt faint. What would a man with all of this want with a girl like me? I thought. There must be other women on his level who can compete with him. I can't do anything for him but be happy he gave me the time of day. Why is he spending so much time with me? I couldn't figure it out. He told me twice that he was glad I could figure things out, but this was beyond me; I had no clue. I wasn't as good as I thought.

There were many beautiful trees all around the house, and in the yard were three gazebos, each as gorgeous as the other.

We drove around to the back of the house, where the driveway stopped. There was another smaller house, and it was not much smaller than the house in front of it. It was beautiful, too. The windows were clear as crystal, not a spot on them. Come to think of it, everything was perfect; nothing was dead or wilted, and it was amazing. He stopped the car and got out. Coming around, he stopped to open the trunk and then walked around to open my door. I got out, trying not to look as if I'd never seen anything as beautiful as this before.

This is an amazing place you have here; it must take a lot to keep it up. Do you have staff? I asked. Yes, there are several staff members here who keep everything I need under control. Now, let's get everything out of the trunk of the car," he said. I walked around and looked in; it was packed with all sorts of things. There was a big picnic basket a very nice tablecloth, plates, glasses, and another bag with a blanket. There was a large umbrella with a base for shade. Wow, he's thought of everything.

We took everything out of the car, then I headed to the house. No! Not that way, we're going this way, he yelled. Turning around, I followed him to a massive shade tree. He put the umbrella and its base to the side, picked up the bag with the blanket, and then spread it on the ground. He placed the picnic basket on the blanket, then he put the tablecloth on top of it, and all the other things were put in their places. Looking at me, he said, "You can sit down now. He took my hand and helped me onto the blanket, then he helped me to the ground. Thank you, I said, and looked around again. I couldn't help but look around at my surroundings. He sat next to me and took out a bottle of wine. I had never tasted wine before, but I wasn't about to tell him that. Then he picked up two glasses, poured a little into each, and passed one to me. I smelled it like I had seen the people do on TV before they took a sip. It smelled very bitter, as if it would have a bitter taste. I didn't want to put it in my mouth, but he took a sip of his, and I didn't want to disappoint him, so I sipped a little of mine. It was horrible.

I couldn't help looking around again; this place was too much. I pinched my arm to see if I was dreaming; it hurt, so I knew I wasn't. I found myself doing that a lot lately.

"These are some very exquisite houses, and your yard is to die for," I said, again. It's okay," he replied, with no excitement at all.

I'd give anything to have someplace like this to call home, I thought to myself.

"What a wonderful place to picnic! Thank you for sharing it with me," I told him.

"You're welcome; I thought you'd love it," he replied.

"I do. I've never seen anything so beautiful! You have great taste in everything."

"I like nice things," he replied, and that was all he had to say about it..

The landscape and fountains were beautiful, not to mention the houses. I knew they were the most unique I had ever seen.

"Did you design your homes yourself?" I asked.

"Yes, I did," he replied.

"Where did you get the idea for them?" I asked.

"I've encountered many beautiful and unique things, more than I could ever tell you about. I know great things when I see them, and this place is a little bit of all those things I've seen in my lifetime of travels," he said.

"Wow! I would give anything to have seen some of the things you've seen and to have experienced so many of the things you have. You're so young to have done so much."

"I'm not as young as I look, and I try to take care of myself. And would you give anything to have all of this?" he asked.

Before I could answer, he changed the subject.

The day turned out to be perfect for a picnic. To my surprise, I couldn't have asked for a more beautiful place to have one.

"Are you hungry yet?" he asked.

"Starved," I replied.

He opened the basket and took out two yellow plates.

"Yellow is your favorite color," he said, as if he were already sure of it.

"Yes, it is. How did you know?"

"Oh, a little bird told me," He said.

"Sure, a little bird told you!" I replied.

He smiled and set the plates on the cloth.

"Today's meal is simple: just some chicken, potato salad, and a few deviled eggs, which I prefer to call stuffed eggs. The 'devil' part doesn't sit well with me," he said, then smiled. "I also brought fruit, and oh, don't let me forget, a couple of sandwiches if you'd like one."

"Sounds great," I replied.

He laid all the food in the containers onto the tablecloth.

"Pick your poison," he said.

I took a little of everything, and so did he. We sat and talked. The food was terrific, as always. Afterward, we lay back on the blanket. The tree branches blocked the sky as we looked up. He asked me to get up for a minute, and then he put everything away and moved the blanket to an open spot where we could look up at the sky without it being blocked.

We began to tell each other what the clouds looked like to each of us.

"I see a swan over there and a bunny over there," I said.

"I see it! I think that one looks like a fish, and over there is a face," he said.

"Yes, it is," I replied.

This was a truly special day, and I got to rest while having a great time.

"Aiden, do you visit this place often?" I asked.

"Only on special occasions," he replied.

"Is this a special occasion?" I asked.

"Of course," he replied. "Enjoy your day, and the next time we come, I'll show you the houses."

"That would be nice, but right now, I want to enjoy it," I said.

We lay there laughing and talking. He talked the most since we met. I thought he had such a wonderful laugh, and I was happy to hear it. He always seemed so serious most of the time, but today, he let go, which was great. He discussed his travels and the people he had met. I told him more about my boring life, and he thought it interesting. I didn't know why. My life wasn't exciting, but I could live with it if he found it fascinating.

Before we knew it, it was over in the evening, and it was time to drive back to the city. He loaded up the car and walked me around the grounds before we left. It was even more beautiful close-up.

"Thank you, Aiden, for another lovely day. Today was unbelievable, and I will never forget it. You are an amazing person, and I am enjoying every moment I spend with you."

"I feel the same," he replied. "Today was terrific, and you were the perfect date. I enjoy your company so much," he said.

And then it happened! He took me in his arms, looked me in the eyes, and there it was again. Something happened. His eyes were different, and they looked strange! I thought I saw something scary in them, but I didn't have time to think about it because he kissed me like I had never been kissed before. I'd waited for days for this kiss. I felt like I was sixteen years old again and knew I was in love with Aiden.

I wished I knew how he felt about me. If only he loved me as much as I loved him, everything I had dreamed could come true. If only he loved me too, I thought, as he kissed me.

When he let me go, he asked if I would consider being the most precious person in his life. My eyes lit up, and I said, "Yes! Of course I will, if you're sure you want me," I screamed.

"I'm as sure as I ever will be. I want you more than you'll ever know," he said.

My heart almost exploded with joy. He wants me! He wants me for his own! I'd wanted this since I saw him that night at church! Now he's mine, and I'm his. I no longer have to worry. It all worked out! As I wanted, we kissed again and walked to the car.

It took three and a half hours to get back home, but for some reason, it didn't feel as long as it had when we were coming. We talked until we arrived at my house, and by the time we got there, it was late.

He walked me to the door and unlocked it. For the first time, since we've met, he kissed me goodnight on the porch and walked back to the car. He waved goodbye and drove off.

I went inside in a daze and got ready for bed. With all that had happened today on my mind. I lay down on my bed, and suddenly, my eyes and stomach felt horrible. I rubbed my belly, turned over, and closed my eyes. It will be hard to sleep tonight. My mind would be full of wonderful thoughts of my Aiden, which sounded terrific.

My stomach had been hurting for a long time. I began to think I should get up and take something for it, but it was a different kind of hurt. It was like the feeling you get when you know something is wrong, but you do it anyway. But I wasn't doing anything wrong, so why was I having these feelings? Not just tonight, but for the last five days?

I found myself very confused. There was no need to try to figure it out because, as far as I was concerned, nothing was wrong. Everything was right, and everything was going just as I had prayed and hoped it would go.

So, with that thought, I got up, put on my pajamas, brushed my hair and teeth, and went to bed, hoping I could get some relief and sleep.

Day Six

I woke up the next morning, trying to solve the mystery of the lingering sickness in my stomach; after a few minutes, it always went away, but this was the first time it had lingered overnight and into the next morning. I went to work feeling unwell and very uneasy, almost as if something inside me was all wrong. It was an extraordinary feeling, and I couldn't clear my mind all morning; despite my desire to feel better, it continued to linger. My stomach felt like it was going to empty at any moment. From information others had told me, and if I didn't know better, I would have thought I was pregnant, but knowing I hadn't been with a man before, I knew that wasn't possible, and I knew it wasn't a miraculous act from God, so that thought was quickly dismissed. But what could be wrong with me? Maybe I'm coming down with something; perhaps I've caught a bug. Yes, that's it! I've caught a bug, I thought. I'd better stop at the drugstore on my way home and pick up something to stop whatever it is before it gets too bad.

Today was busy; many people called to schedule vacations, and the phone continued to ring. I had no time to feel sick; work was hectic! I had no time to think of anything but work, and the lunch break was well-welcomed. I was worn out. Getting up from my desk, I wondered what I could eat to make my stomach feel better. I didn't want to eat anything, but something might help. I decided on soup and crackers from the diner on the corner. As a young child, my mom would always give me soup and crackers when I had a stomachache or a cold, which seemed to help alleviate the symptoms. While eating my soup and crackers, my mind drifted to Aiden for the first time that day.

Come to think of it, he hadn't called me yet, and he hadn't told me last night what we were doing tonight. It was unusual. He always told me what we'd do the next day the night before, so I'd have some idea of what to expect. However, he didn't mention anything about it last night. Finishing my soup and looking at my watch, it was almost time to return to work. Believe it or not, the soup did help a little, or so I thought.

Walking back to work, I doubled over with pain! This was ridiculous! I'd never had such pain in my stomach before in my life. Something is very wrong, I thought. I need to make myself a doctor's appointment. Maybe there's something more to this than I'm thinking. I needed to see my doctor. I decided to call and make an appointment as soon as I returned to my office. After calling, they scheduled me for the coming Monday, but since it was only Friday, I had to wait another two and a half days. Hopefully, I can make it until then, I thought. My cell phone rang after I talked to my doctor's office about my appointment. It was Aiden. "Hello, bright eyes, how are you today?" he asked. "Not so good, I'm feeling sick today," I told him. "Sick? What seems to be the problem?" he asked. "I don't know, it's just a lot of pain and nervousness in my stomach," I said. "Do you think it can be the result of all the rich foods you've eaten in the last few days?" he asked. "I don't think it's the food, it feels very different from what I'm used to. I think it's something else. I'm not sure what it is. I have an appointment with my doctor on Monday. Hopefully, I can make it until then."

"I was thinking of you earlier today. You didn't tell me last night what you had planned for tonight," I said. "Since you're not feeling well, what if I just come to your place and make you a light meal? Then you can rest." "Wow! That would be wonderful! I don't feel like doing too much tonight, and I would love a nice bowl of your soup if that's not too much to ask." "Sure, it isn't. I'll make enough to last for a day or two." "Thank you, Aiden, what would I do without you?" He laughed, and the work phone rang. "I've got to return to work; will seven be ok for you to come by?" I asked. "Yes, seven is fine. I'll see you then." We said goodbye and hung up. I scheduled vacations for the entire afternoon into the evening. Today was hectic. We hadn't had a day like this in a few months. I was glad because it took my mind off my stomach. I took my last call around four forty-five. It took me fifteen minutes to schedule my last customer's vacation, and I was out the door by five. I had to catch up on a few things I hadn't had time to do yesterday, like cleaning my kitchen. Aiden's kitchen was spotless, while mine was a mess of dishes, since I never had time to wash them. I decided I needed to clean it up before he arrived.

When I got home, I started cleaning right away. I had hoped he would bring what he needed for the soup, because my fridge was always empty. I cleaned the kitchen and put everything in its place. After that, I went into the living room and tidied it up a bit; the house wasn't in too bad shape. I just wanted it to be clean when Aiden arrived.

Walking up the stairs, I had to stop and catch my breath. Rubbing my stomach, I could barely reach the top. I was fine six days ago. This had suddenly come on, and it hasn't stopped since the night at the singles party. What could I have eaten or drunk to make me feel this way? Maybe I've gotten food poisoning from something I ate or drank, but whatever it was, it was hurting me with a vengeance. Still feeling bad, I jumped into the shower. I didn't feel like washing or flat-ironing my hair, so I kept it dry, making the shower quick, which seemed to be all I could do nowadays.

I got out of the shower, put on my pajamas, and a robe. He will have to deal with this tonight. I didn't feel like getting dressed and then undressed again anyway. He knew I wasn't feeling well. I intended to go straight to bed when he left. I hoped that the soup was as good as everything else he made for me; it might make me feel much better. I grabbed a blanket and a pillow, took them downstairs, unlocked the front door, and then made myself comfortable on the couch. It felt so good to relax for a few minutes: no phones, no people, no noise, just complete silence. Looking at my watch, I had thirty minutes to relax and enjoy the peace, something I hadn't had in a while.

I woke up to the sound of the doorbell ringing. "Who's there?" I yelled. "Aiden," he called back. "Come on in, the door is open!" He came in with two bags in his arms. "How do you feel, bright eyes?" he asked. "I'm a little better. I'm lying here, trying to stay still and relax." "Good girl! Lay there and rest. Point me to the kitchen, and I'll start the soup." I pointed him toward the kitchen. "Go until you see it," I told him. He walked in the direction I pointed, and I closed my eyes and passed out again. I woke again to the most wonderful smells coming from the kitchen. It was all I could do to wait for it to finish. It also smelled like bread was baking. He can't be baking fresh bread, but it smelled like it, I thought.

I sat up and turned on the TV, flipping through the channels. I stumbled across a movie that seemed very peaceful and family-oriented, so I decided to watch it. After about an hour, Aiden came in and asked how I was feeling and if I thought I could eat anything. "I'm feeling the same. And yes, I think I can eat something. Whatever it is, it smells terrific," I said. "It will be ready shortly. I will bring it to you. Don't worry about getting up," he said. "Thank you, Aiden. I'm thrilled you're here with me. I'm sorry I couldn't cook for you, but I'll make it up to you when I'm feeling better." "No problem," he replied, and then went back into the kitchen. Looking back at the TV, I had no clue what was happening in the movie. It was already playing when I turned it on, and I had fallen asleep while watching it. I turned it off and lay down. I had imagined this for days: Aiden and I were here in our home together, a family taking care of each other and loving each other forever. Even though this was what I had imagined, we could have it together. I wondered if he thought about it as much as I did. He never said it to me, but I hoped he felt the same way. He did ask me, however, to be his girlfriend, and that's a great start. I lay there thinking how great it would be to have this house full of our kids, hearing them laugh and play, and he and I being so proud of them and of ourselves for doing such a great job with them - two girls and two boys - our lives would be perfect.

Aiden interrupted my thoughts. "Dinner is served," he said, and he asked if anyone was hungry. "I'm starving," I replied. He set the food on the coffee table and helped me arrange it. "I hope you don't mind chicken noodle soup with homemade crackers," he said. "Oh no! I'm sure I don't! You made crackers? I thought I smelled some bread baking. You are terrific, Aiden!" He handed me a napkin and said, "I'll be back in a minute, then we can eat together." I told him I would wait for him. He came back with his food on a tray and sat next to me. "You may not want to sit too close, I'm not sure what's going on with me, and I don't want you to get sick," I told him. "I'm not worried about getting sick; I never get sick. I'm in the best shape of my life," he said. "Never?" I asked. "Never, and you'd better eat before your soup gets cold," he replied. I tasted the chicken noodle soup and wasn't disappointed. It was heavenly, and the crackers were excellent, too. "Aiden, you have outdone yourself again! Please teach me to cook like this, then I can make some delicious meals for you. You are the best cook I know." "Thank you, Alex. Now eat your soup so you can feel better." We finished our dinner, and he took all the dishes and trays back to the kitchen. I didn't hear him washing them, but after a meal like that, he didn't have to clean them. I would be happy to wash them tomorrow when I feel better. He came back and sat down on the other end of the couch. "Alex, lay your head here in my lap and relax," he said.

Is he really going to let me put my head on his lap? At that point, I could hear the children playing throughout the house again in my mind. This is what I want, I thought, if we could only stay this close to each other for the rest of our lives. I lay my head onto his lap, and as soon as I did, my body trembled from the same force I felt before when he held my hand! I tried not to let on, but it was hard; something was going on with Aiden.

I was convinced that every time he touched me, some strange feeling entered me. I've heard of crazy, but this was ridiculous; I took it as a sure sign we were meant for each other. I kept my head there, hoping it would disappear soon, and shortly after, it did, and all was well again. I felt much better after putting my head on his lap; the pain and sickness had all disappeared. I didn't know if the soup or Aiden made me feel better; I didn't understand or care. It felt great to lie beside him with my head in his lap.

"Do you think you will be able to go out tomorrow?" he asked.

"If I keep feeling as well as I do now, I can do anything tomorrow."

"Would you like to find a movie to watch on TV?" he asked. "If so, I will find one for us. You lie here and relax," he said.

He flipped through the channels and found an old classic, "Old Yeller." I told him I've always loved that movie and that it was okay.

"Are you sure?" he asked.

"I can't think of a better one," I replied with a smile. We watched the movie and discussed parts of it, and all the while, I felt myself feeling better and better. His being near me made me feel good. All the strange feelings went away. I felt great. My recovery was remarkable.

I sat up, looked at Aiden, and said, "I feel like a new person. What was in that soup?"

"Just a lot of my kind of love for you," he replied.

"His kind of love for me... he must have loved me a lot because that soup had me feeling like I was never going to be sick again. I don't know what you put in it, but I feel much better. Thank you, Aiden, for coming over and caring for me, because I felt terrible."

"You're welcome anytime," he replied.

I lay my head on his shoulder, and we finished *Old Yeller*.

After the movie, we sat and discussed my busy day at work. I told him how much it took to stay through the whole shift. I was glad I did because I couldn't afford to lose another day's pay, even though Aiden had kept his word, giving me triple the salary for the eight hours he asked me to miss. It helped me catch up on some bills I was behind on.

I asked how his week had gone.

"Okay, I guess. Sometimes you win some, and sometimes you lose some," he replied.

"Did you lose some of your patients, or did you gain some?" I asked.

"I gained some, and I lost some. The ones I've gained, I'm not worried about, but the ones I've lost, I'm not happy about."

Most of the time, when Aiden talked about things, he wasn't clear. I always found myself trying to figure out what he was talking about. One thing I didn't like about him was that he was never clear in conversations; it was like he didn't want me to understand.

"I hope you can win the ones back you lost," I said.

"Oh, it's just a matter of time," he replied.

I wasn't clear about what that meant, so I left it alone.

I wished I could ask him a question and have him give me a simple answer, but I didn't think he ever would. It was hard to have a conversation with him where I had clarity on any subject we discussed. This must be how he is, and if so, I could live with it. If this is the only fault I could find in him, it was nothing. What does it matter if he speaks in riddles? I was good at figuring things out. He had said so himself.

"Would you like to watch another movie?" I asked.

"No, it's getting late, and you need to get some rest. I've already cleaned the kitchen and put the rest of the soup in the refrigerator. The crackers are in a Ziplock bag on the counter, and there's juice and fruit in the fridge as well, if you need or want it later."

"Thank you, Aiden. You are my knight in shining armor. You've been my lifesaver."

"No problem. Bright eyes, I'm going to go now so that you can rest. If you feel like it tomorrow, we should do something together, okay?" he said.

"Okay, I'm sure I'll feel fine tomorrow," I replied.

He stood up, and so did I.

"I'll walk you to the door," I told him.

"No need. I know my way out, and I'll put the lock on for you. You go upstairs and get some rest."

He hugged and kissed me, then said, "Goodnight."

"Thanks again for everything. I feel like my old self again," I told him.

"No problem. Get some rest now," he said.

I gathered up my blanket and pillow and then headed upstairs. What a great night! I felt so much better. It's incredible what the proper soup can do for you. I needed that, and I needed some rest.

Aiden had shown me such kindness. How could I ever repay him? I always thought of him and hoped he thought of me as he lay in his bed each night. He was such a special person to me. I hoped to show him that one day.

Pulling the covers over my head, I closed my eyes and fell asleep with Aiden on my mind.

Day Seven

Aiden called me early to see if I was feeling better and if I wanted to go check out the house he owned in the country, where we had had the picnic; if so, we would go out later this morning. It was supposed to be another warm day, and I was off work, so I agreed. "What time would you be coming by to pick me up?" I asked.

"Let's make it early, how about nine?" He said. "That will be great; I'll see you then and take care I replied."

"Yes, I'll see you later this morning." "And the same goes for you," he said. We hung up, and I did a few things around the house during the couple of hours I had, doing as much as possible, which wasn't much, but it looked a little neater than before. Looking over at the clock, it was already ten minutes past eight; my life seemed to be passing me by; time was never on my side; every time I looked at a clock, time had passed by so quickly. I'd better get ready; with not much time to spare, I followed my routine: a quick shower, my hair pulled back, and something comfortable to wear. This was beginning to feel normal for me; I didn't have much time for anything but Aiden and work. I found myself calling out of work, which was something I didn't do. Even work was beginning to be affected by my new relationship. I wasn't too worried about it, though. If things kept going the way they were, I might not even have to work; I could stay home and be the wife of Aiden Summers and the mother of his children. The thought of that made me happy. I smiled and continued to get ready. He would be here soon, and I didn't want to make him wait.

By the time I was completely ready, the doorbell rang; I walked over and opened the door. "Good morning, bright eyes," he said.

"Good morning," I replied. "Are you ready? We have a long drive ahead; I'd like to arrive early enough to give you a tour." This was the most excited I had ever seen him. I'm ready to go, "just let me grab my sweater and the key."

"Today promises to be glorious; there is so much to accomplish. I feel good about today," he said. "I've accomplished a lot in the last few weeks and have just a few more loose ends to tie up, and my mission will be complete."

"I'm glad you finished everything except the loose ends," I told him.

"Oh, that's alright. That's nothing," he said. "I'll wrap them up by the end of the day." He seemed pretty sure about his loose ends; how would he wrap them up if we spent the day together? I wondered. The houses in the country were such beautiful homes. I could imagine Aiden and me living there with three or four kids running around in that unbelievable yard. We would be so happy there; I would be the perfect wife and mother.

I hadn't seen inside the house, but I could picture the kitchen; it must be huge! I thought. The kitchen in his home, which was not far from me, was big, but this one might be able to fit two of those kitchens in it; the house in the country was a massive mansion, not a house. I could imagine the rooms in that place! Every bedroom should have its own bathroom, considering the available space. I would love a huge walk-in closet. I don't have a lot of clothes, but if I were to marry Aiden, I'd have lots of clothes and everything else. I felt happy just thinking about it.

"A penny for your thoughts," I heard him shouting, bringing me back from daydreaming.

"I'm sorry, I was enjoying this beautiful drive; it's such a lovely morning," I replied.

"Yes, it is, and it will only get better from here on," he said. I looked over at him and smiled.

After three hours of driving, we arrived at the large bronze gate. He parked and got out to unlock it, just as he had done before, and then we drove in. Everything looked even more beautiful today than it had the day before. I think it was all because I knew now how Aiden felt about me; he had asked me the last time I was here to be that special someone in his life, and I had agreed, so this time, coming here meant a lot to me. I will always hold this place deeply in my heart. We drove to the house, parked the car, and got out. "Let's look at the house in the back first," he said.

"Sure," I replied, and we walked about a hundred feet. He unlocked the door and said, "After you, my dear," and moved out of the way for me to enter. I stepped inside and looked around; it was just amazing! Wow! It was lovely; everything was bright and cheery, with colors on the inside that I particularly liked. It was nice and clean, and the kitchen was huge, fully stocked with modern appliances and a variety of food. He showed me around; everything was of the highest quality, and I had never seen anything like it before. I was stunned by the beauty of the place; I thought all of this would soon be mine. He showed me all the rooms and baths; they were lovely! Then he said, "Let's go to the big house."

"Sure, I can't wait to see it," I replied. We walked back towards the big house, and I got a good look at it; it was made of the most exquisite material, and the architecture was superb.

I was amazed at its beauty; this place was like nothing I'd ever seen before; the beauty was unbelievable. I hoped I wouldn't pass out once he opened the door and I looked inside.

"You wouldn't," he said.

"I won't what?" I asked.

"You won't pass out when you get inside," he said. I looked at him with a surprised look. How did he know what I was thinking? "I want you to see everything I have to offer you, and I'll make sure you see it all," he said. Then he opened the door, and I went in, finding it hard to breathe. The place was much more than I could ever imagine; the house in the back was a sight to behold! But this! Words could not even begin to describe it! I couldn't say a word; I looked around with my mouth wide open. My eyes couldn't believe what they were seeing. This was too good to be true, I thought to myself. I could never have anything like this, and something had to be wrong. I felt something just wasn't right with all of this; it didn't make sense to me. A short while later, I got that gut feeling again. I felt like I was going to throw up; I turned and ran back outside, leaning over the porch; it felt like my whole insides were coming out onto the ground below! He came out to the porch and asked if I was okay. He began to rub my back.

"You seem a little overwhelmed; maybe I shouldn't have brought you back here," he said.

"No! I'm fine. It must have been something I ate this morning that didn't agree with me. I'm okay now. Let's continue our tour, shall we?" I asked.

"Sure, if you're okay."

I took a deep breath and went back inside; my mind started to wander again. What would someone with so much want with someone like me? I have nothing to offer him; what does he see in me that makes him want to share all he has with me? It doesn't make sense; most successful people want to collaborate with others to achieve more, but he has chosen me without any significant contribution to make. It seemed strange, but it's everything anyone could ever wish for; maybe I'm just lucky! Yes, perhaps I should look at it that way: I'm fortunate he chose me; after all, the room was full of women to choose from, and he picked me, me! Out of all the women, I'm the one he decided he wanted; he must have seen something in me. I made myself content with that thought.

As I mentioned earlier, we continued to view the house; there were no words to describe it! The stained glass with the sun shining through was excellent and impressive. The colors were showcased throughout the house, and the open spaces featured a multitude of colors emanating from the other stained-glass windows; it was truly a sight to behold. I was breathless. He took me by the hand and led me out to the side of the house, a side I had not seen before. It had a large, very well-kept garden, and my eyes widened - a garden! I love gardens!

"And it's so large, is this where you get your produce for the meals you cooked for me?" I asked.

"Yes," he said, "it's all grown here."

"I must have died and gone to heaven," I thought! Died, and gone to heaven is what I've done!

"Do you like it here?" he asked.

"Like it! Oh, Aiden! Who could ask for such a beautiful place? I love it. You have done so well for yourself; I'm proud of you." He took me by the hand and asked if I wanted to share everything with him.

"Are you sure you want me to share this with you? I have nothing to offer you, nothing at all," I replied.

"All I need to know is if you are sure you want this."

"All I need is you! You alone will do; I don't need anything else but you," he replied, then took me in his arms. All I could say was,

"Yes, this is what I want; you are what I want." Then I kissed him, and the deal was sealed as far as I was concerned; Aiden was mine, and now I knew for certain I was his.

All of this, all that he had, he was willing to share with me, someone who had nothing, now had everything. I could never wish for more. I thought about Liz, my best friend and sister.

"Wait until I tell her what has happened, she won't believe it! She will say, 'Wow! This was quick. Are you sure this is what you want?'" I would say, "I couldn't be more confident." She would grab me and give me a big hug, saying how happy she was for me, and wish me all the happiness in the world. I would then invite her out as soon as possible to visit and have dinner with Aiden and me; she was more than welcome at our home whenever she felt like being there. Who knows, I might even ask her to move in with us.

All these thoughts ran through my mind as he held me tight. He finally let me go and led me to a room he had not shown me earlier. It was a large room set up just like the cinema Liz and I had visited, but it was much bigger and more extravagant.

"I've set up a movie for us to watch if that's okay with you," he said.

"Yes, it's fine," I replied. We sat down. Then he pressed a button, and a screen came up.

"Would you like some popcorn and a soda?"

"Sure, this was just like being at the movies, only better. Here, you didn't have to listen to all the noisy people who talked during the show; this was a welcome change." He got up to get popcorn and soda. I sat down and watched as the movie started. The title came across the screen: *Do you remember this?* Was the movie's name.

"I don't think I've ever seen this one," I yelled over to Aiden.

"Oh! I'm sure you have; when you see it, you'll remember," he yelled back to me from across the room.

"Is it a new one?" I yelled back at him.

"No! It's not new," he said.

"I've never heard of it," I thought.

"It should interest you," he told me as he handed me a box of popcorn and a soda.

"What's it about?" I asked.

"If I tell you, it won't be a surprise, will it?" he said.

"You're right, Aiden, what was I thinking?"

Liz and I had seen almost every movie out there, but I guess we missed this one; he sat back down, and the movie started to play; it began with a woman and her husband in a delivery room of a hospital; the woman was giving birth to their first child, she was having a difficult time with the delivery, her husband was coaching her through it, and he was doing a great job. He seemed focused on his wife and the troubles she was experiencing. Just breathe, breathe, honey; you can do it, honey! He told her; she did as he said, and soon a baby girl was born to them! How sweet, "I said," they have a beautiful daughter; how proud they must be. As we continued watching the movie, more and more things began to happen that reminded me of my mother and father; even the little girl was a lot like me. As she grew older, I became more interested in it. Many things that happen in their family are the exact things that happen in my family. It was weird; it's like he's found an old movie of my family. I looked over at him, and he was so engrossed in the film that he didn't notice me watching him; he seemed to be thoroughly enjoying it.

I started watching the movie again, and I could have fallen out of my seat! The more I watched, the more I realized this was a movie of my life! What and how can this be possible? I jumped up, yelling, "Where did you get this movie? Where did it come from?" He looked over at me and said, "What's wrong? Don't you enjoy watching yourself on film?"

"What is all this?" I yelled!

"And again, where did you get this?"

He stood up, looked at me with this sinister smile, and said, "I got it from you! Got it from me! I never gave you this."

"Oh yes, you did," he replied. "No, I didn't! I've never given you anything!" I yelled. "Really? Are you sure about that?" Then he started to laugh uncontrollably! Then, just like that, he stopped. He said, "You've given me everything, you have." "What in this world are you talking about?" I asked!

"What have I given you?" "Everything!" He yelled, "The day you turn your back on your so-called God! You gave me everything!" I looked at him, and he seemed to change before my eyes; he was no longer the handsome guy I had met; his whole countenance changed. It was wicked, and I became terrified! What was happening? My life was still flashing across the screen, and it was everything I had ever done, good and bad, even the things I didn't want others to know about or see were there. "Look at it!" He yelled!

"You have been a bad girl! And now you're mine."

"I'm not yours," I yelled! "Yes, you are mine! You gave yourself to me years ago; you walked away from the only one who could help you, even your friend Liz. Liz tried to help you, but you didn't listen to her! You wanted me," he screamed! "I didn't want you! I didn't even know it was you!"

"Oh yes, you did; even before we met at the church that night, you wanted me. Anytime you weren't in contact with that God of yours, it let me know you wanted me."

I grabbed my head; this can't be happening! I shouted! "Oh, it's happening! And there's nothing you can do to stop it," he shouted. I began to cry. "Please take me home," I asked. "Home, you are home! Remember, you have confirmed twice that this is what you wanted; now it's all yours! You should have been more careful with your choices; humans are all alike, and material things get you all the time." He grabbed my arm and dragged me into the kitchen. I struggled to free myself, but he was too strong, and I was too weak; I could do nothing.

"You humans are so easy! All of you want to be herded like cattle and sheep to the slaughter! You want to be told what to do, when to do it, and how to do it. You want others to think for you! You are too lazy to think for yourself or use the brain God gave you to make the right decisions. You are all so self-centered; everything is always about you! You never think of others, how you can help, or lighten their loads; you want everything your neighbor has! You cheat on your spouses! You steal from each other! You kill each other like you change your clothes! And life means nothing to you. You don't forgive each other; you hold grudges as if you have never hurt, mistreated, lied to, or stabbed someone in the back; you act as if you are perfect and everyone else is a sinner! You mistreat each other so efficiently; I don't have to do it for you! But wait, this is the one that gets me the most: some of you don't know if you are men or women. Your children, your children are a lost cause! You haven't taught them of your so-called God, as he informed you to. They are disrespectful, unholy, ungrateful; in other words, they are a disgrace, such a disgrace that I almost don't want them! Those of you who have children and have not taught them about God have been negligent parents. You have not taught your children about God. Your generation is the worst I've gotten yet! All because you're too busy being what everybody else is being; there is no difference between you and my people." Then he laughed and said, "I almost forgot, you are my people! No one cares enough about the other to help or teach them about God; I love that. You don't know how much that means to me, and as far as I'm concerned, I'm going to keep your minds so full of nonsense and keep you so busy that you won't ever have time to think about God! And I'll ensure you never pick up a Bible to read just one verse from it. I have taught you humans well; you always follow my tricks! I am so good; I'm better than good! I don't have to work for your souls; you humans give them to me on a silver platter!" I must pat myself on the back, he said, and he did.

He began to laugh again; it was the worst sound I'd ever heard. He dragged me over to the counter and opened the drawer; as he pulled me closer to him, I pleaded to be let go, but all my pleading was unheard. He looked me in the eye and said, "I will make sure you die in your sin," then I felt a sharp pain in my left side, and again in my back! He let me go, and I fell to the floor. I grabbed my side and then my back; they were wet; I looked at my hands. They were covered in blood. I looked up at him, and he stood there looking down at me with a large knife in his hands; he stood over me with that same sinister smile on his face, the same smile I thought I had seen on many different occasions. I saw the same full-blown wicked look in his eyes that I thought I had seen many times before, but it was fully exhibited this time.

For two or three seconds, I found it very difficult to take even a shallow breath, and then it became clear to me what had happened: he'd stabbed me, and the wounds must have been severe because the pain was unbearable. He wasn't Aiden. I realized I had given myself to Satan, not just in the last few days but in the past also; then he said something to me that hurt much worse than the wounds ever could.

He told me that I should have stuck with God! At least he did love me. "You let this world and all it has to offer blind you! But it's great for me! Now I don't have to burn for you! You were so easy to deceive. Thank you for coming over to the dark side; now I can move on to my next victim, but don't you forget you're mine!" he said. And again, he began to laugh uncontrollably.

I lay there bleeding to death, and all I could think about was what he said, how I had left God and wanted the things of this world. I thought about my father and mother; they were great parents; they taught me of God's love and forgiveness; they didn't fail me in that department; they made sure they took me to church to worship God; we came together in our home to study his word. How disappointed they would be if they could see what had become of me. I never thought I had strayed this far from God, but as I lay there, I realized how far I had strayed from him, so far that I lay at the feet of Satan himself dying, thinking I was in love with a godly and good man, how wrong I was.

Thinking of my dear friend Liz and how hurt she would be to hear of my death, if I should die. She would be devastated. I thought about how often she had invited me back to church, but she always respected my decision not to attend. I thought about my life before I met Aiden; I had a simple but good life. I wanted to start attending church again, but I never had the time; something was always taking up my time, and I didn't have a minute to spare. How disappointed God must be in me. I knew he loved me; it was I who walked away from him, not the other way around. Suddenly, Satan let out the most horrible scream, then told me to hurry up and die! "What are you waiting for?" he asked. He told me there was no hope for me now; I was one less he had to worry about.

I felt myself getting weaker. Looking up at him, he resembled a child with his hand in the candy jar; he was so excited and pleased with himself, with his ego showing boldly. I knew I would be dead soon; I was losing too much blood, and I couldn't stop it; closing my weak eyes, I prayed the last prayer I would pray on this earth. I said, "Dear heavenly Father, I find myself in the worst predicament; I stayed away from you, and all I knew to be right and good. I didn't realize how far I'd gone until today, dear Lord; I've hurt you and many others by not living up to what I knew to be good and honorable in your eyes. Lord, I lie here dying, and no one knows where I am or what's happening to me except you, me, and Satan. I'm at his mercy, and he has none; I need your help; I'm asking for your help; I'm asking for your forgiveness of my sins; I'm asking for your mercy, Lord, help me, I have many sins that need to be forgiven, I'm so sorry for leaving your side, and in my last breaths, I ask that you forgive me with your forgiving mercy and grace. Please save me when you return to gather your people. Help Liz get through this ordeal somehow. Let her know I'll be okay. Somehow, let her know that I've made things right with you. I don't know how you will do it, but I believe you will do all I've asked. Thank you for loving and caring for me throughout my life. I trust you with my life, and I look forward to seeing you soon! In the name of Jesus, I ask, amen."

I opened my eyes, and Satan was still standing over me. I looked at him, and somehow, I got the strength to say, you've made a grave mistake! No mistakes made here; you are mine, he replied, with a great big ugly grin on his face. You see, that's where you're wrong, I shouted. I've just spoken with God. I asked Him to forgive me of all my sins and to take me back to live with Him when He returns. I no longer belong to you! Praise God! I belong to him again, and he has forgiven me. He still loves me! You have no hold on me now! No hold at all! You've lost again! And you will always lose repeatedly!

As long as God is in the business of forgiveness and forgives sins, we humans can ask for His forgiveness. Too bad you didn't have the sense to do so yourself, I told him. He threw up his hands and yelled, No! She's mine! She's mine! You can't take her back after all she's done! She's done too much to be forgiven!! That's not fair! You always forgive them, he shouted.

He looked down at me with so much hatred and quickly left the room; you can't let me have one, he yelled! No matter how much wrong they do! If they ask for forgiveness with all their heart! You always forgive them, he cried, leaving the room. Closing my eyes, I thanked God again for forgiving me; I knew he had, because I'd asked him to with all my heart. Feeling weak from loss of blood, I thought to myself that no one could help me, and I was unable to help myself. The only thing I could think of was, by God's grace, someone would show up who could help. Again, I asked for his help; please send someone to find me. Lord, I don't want to die here alone. My eyes were closed; I seemed too weak to open them. Trying to move was a bad idea; the pain was unbearable; he must have cut me deep, I thought! My body was in shock; I felt as if the knife had gone completely through both my back and side, and then everything went black. The next thing I remember was hearing someone calling out to me, 'Miss!' Miss! Can you hear me? Miss! Can you hear me? I awakened to someone kneeling over me; I couldn't speak. I was too weak, and all I could do was thank God in my thoughts for sending someone to help! God, you are so merciful and loving.

After a few minutes, I heard sirens. He had already called an ambulance, and they were on their way. For the first time since Satan stabbed me, I felt I might live through this if I could only get to the hospital in time.

God must love me and have a plan for my life, I thought. The paramedics rushed in and began working on me; I heard one tell the other, I'm surprised she's still alive; look at all the blood she's lost; we must stop that bleeding. After working on me for a while, they put me on the bed and rushed me out the door. We arrived at the hospital, and I was rushed into an emergency room; the doctor looked at my wounds, stopped the bleeding, and decided to get X-rays. When the X-rays came back, the doctor came in and told me I was fortunate. He told me my left lung was completely sliced in half, but each half somehow still held air and worked as if it were never damaged.

It's unexplainable; I've never seen or heard of anything like this. You're lucky, he told me again. I wished I could speak; I wanted to say to him, 'Luck had nothing to do with this. God!' My loving father had spared my life; and he alone had saved me. I wanted to shout, 'He saved me!' Repeatedly, he saved me! I was then informed that surgery was needed to repair my left lung and the wound in my back.

He asked for my permission to operate, and all I could do was nod my head in agreement. Do you have anyone we can call? He asked. My mind fell on Liz, but I was too weak to give them her number, so I shook my head no; I would tell them about her after surgery and after I rested for a while. We must prepare you for surgery, the doctor told me. I nodded my head, and he left the room. The pain was still unbearable; they hadn't given anything for it yet. I lay there, hoping that someone would come in and knock me out with a strong medication; I just wanted the pain to stop!

Again, I asked for God's help; soon, the nurse came in to put in another IV; the excitement was overwhelming; I began to cry; my thoughts went to Liz and what would happen if I didn't make it, she would be heartbroken, and I wouldn't even get to say goodbye to her, the thought was too much for me to bear.

Thinking of something else, I tried to focus on what the nurse was doing to prepare me for surgery. Again, my mind fell on God, God, help me to make it through surgery and give the Doctor wisdom to repair my lung. Thank you again, Father, for keeping the air moving; I don't know how you did it, but I'm grateful! Just keep me as you already have; I trust you.

The nurse completed her task of preparing me for surgery; she walked over to my bed and said, "You have been through a lot, but you have made it this far, I'm sure you can make it through this last major ordeal, you are a strong young lady, you have determination, and youth on your side, you will be okay." I tried to smile, but I felt it didn't come out quite right.

Soon after, another nurse came in to take me down to the operating room, transferring me from one bed to the other. I tried again to smile, but I wasn't sure if I had or not. I was grateful for all they were doing to help me, and I wanted to show my appreciation. Soon after, she unlocked the bed and started pulling it out of the room; closing my eyes, I thought, this is it, Lord, please go before me, prepare the way, help all to go well, keep me safe, and help my doctor to be led by your hand in Jesus' name. Amen. A peaceful feeling came over me, and I wasn't afraid; I knew God was with me. I could feel it in my heart; I would make it through this.

Entering the operating room, I was at peace, in perfect peace; I knew I would be ok, whether I lived or died. I had faith; he had forgiven me, and if I died, I knew I would have a place with him when he returned. If I lived, I would live for him the rest of my life. This ordeal taught me some important lessons: things I thought were important weren't, being a part of the world wasn't worth sacrificing my soul, and choosing a partner instead of waiting for God to send me one was a grave mistake. But leaving God's side and his instructions were the biggest mistakes I could have ever made. I wanted to come through this to show God how much I love Him and appreciate Him giving me another chance. I want to live with and for him for the rest of my life. The nurse came over, inserted something into my IV, and instructed me to count backward from ten to one. I started counting:

ten, nine, eight, and the next thing I knew, I woke up with a nurse calling my name, 'Alexandra!' Alexandra! Alexandra! It's time to wake up! Wake up! "Are you awake?" she asked. I slowly opened my eyes, and the room was fuzzy. Where am I? I asked, "You're in the hospital, don't you remember?" She replied. Oh yeah, now I remember. I tried to move, but the pain was still unbearable. Don't move! It would be best if you stayed still for now," the nurse shouted. "You've been through a major ordeal, but you did great. The doctor will be in soon to check on you." Closing my eyes again, I thanked God for bringing me through surgery safely. I had prayed more in the last week than in the past few years.

It felt good to talk to God the way I used to; I felt close to Him whenever I prayed. He had taken such good care of me, and even when I strayed, He was still by my side. If he had left me, I wouldn't be alive today. Realizing how much God loved me made me love him back, and I was sorry for the way I'd lived my life in the past years.

Things are going to be different now.

My pain wouldn't stop! I asked the nurse if I could have something for it. "Sure," she replied. She put some pain medication in my IV, and shortly, it started to work. I was relieved, and it was nice to feel comfortable finally. Soon after the meds, I was taken to my room; "Let's get you into bed, careful now; you don't want to hurt yourself; let me help you as much as possible," she told me. I couldn't have helped her if I wanted to. I was too weak and sleepy.

Transferring me to my bed, she said, "You know the police will come in soon to get a report on what happened to you." I thought about what had happened to me. How could I tell them Satan did this to me? They would think I was crazy; they would put me in a mental hospital. That would be precisely what they would do to me if I told them that story. What could I tell them? Convictions made me know I must tell the truth, no matter how crazy it sounded. I wasn't looking forward to it, but it had to be done. Making up my mind to surrender my life back to Christ was the most important thing I could think of, and that meant always telling the truth, no matter how it made me look.

Later, I found the strength to thank the nurse for her loving care; she had been so kind, and I felt she cared about what happened to me. The anesthesia they used to sedate me was very much present in my system; I started to nod off again. I was pleased and grateful to have made it through. I couldn't keep my eyes open; I could feel myself drifting back to sleep. 'You go ahead and rest,' she told me. 'You have some long days ahead; you'll need all the rest you can get.' I tried to smile, then passed out.

I stayed in the hospital for three months, fighting for my life. Somehow, my best friend Liz heard I was there and came to see me; she never left my side, I was told. When we finally saw each other, we cried tears of joy together. I was so glad to see her. My mind ran back to how many times she'd asked me to come with her to church, how many times she'd told me how much Jesus loved me and was waiting with open arms to take me back, if I ever wanted to return to Him. We embraced each other for an extended period, and she told me that she had been praying for me much more intensely over the past weeks than ever before; something had told her that I needed prayer to find the strength to make it through the weeks ahead.

Little did she know she was right. I needed God's mercy and grace to bring me through this horrible experience that I found myself in. I needed him then, and I needed him now, to continue getting me completely through it; I wasn't out of the woods yet, but I could see the light at the edge of it.

Liz never said, 'I told you so,' or 'you went too far.' She never said you should have been praying more, nor that you should have listened. None of those things came from her lips. She only said, 'I love you,' and you know Jesus loves you more than you'll ever know. I knew what she said was the truth, and for the first time in my life, I now believed it with all my heart and soul.

I understand now how much Jesus does love not just me but everyone; my ordeal was a terrible one, and it almost cost me my life and my salvation. I played around on Satan's playground for far too long, to the point I belonged to him. He was more than willing to have me no matter what, and he wasn't willing to give me up without a fight, even if it meant taking my life to make sure he had me in his grip forever.

My life had been only about me and what I wanted; I didn't think anything like this would ever happen to me. I thought I had plenty of time to come back to Christ. I was young, foolish, and selfish, and I thought my life would last forever. Little did I know I was playing with the powers of darkness.

Satan disguises himself as many things, and for me, it was a life partner and material things. He led me to believe that I had found everything I ever wanted or needed in him, but in the end, I paid for giving myself to him.

Praise God for Christian parents, who taught me early on to pray and trust in God. They also studied the Bible with me at home every day, and we went to church every week. Thank God for a true friend who never condemned me for leaving the church or God, but was always there for me when I needed her. She loved me unconditionally and constantly reminded me that Jesus loved me more than I could ever know. Where would I be now if it had not been for these people? I would be lost if it weren't for God and His loving grace and forgiveness.

I consider myself blessed among many, and my life has been spared to be a witness to others who are headed down the same road I traveled. A road that looks so inviting, so lovely, a road that you think will lead you to all you will ever need or want, this road is just a disguise. It's a well-planned one by the master of disguises, designed to trap you. It's a plan to entangle you so tight you will never be able to free yourself, a plan to keep you in his grip until he can do the unthinkable to you.

I have traveled this road and can tell you from my mistakes that it's not the road you want to take. This road leads to destruction; I travelled willingly, looking for what I already had. Everything I ever needed, I already had, and I walked away from what I already had, looking for what I thought was even better; I was wrong.

This road will destroy you like it almost destroyed me; you are not strong enough to travel it; there is nothing you can do once you start this journey; this road takes a firm hold on you, and without God's help, you will never be able to leave it alive!

I'm telling you my story, so you don't travel on the same road that only leads to destruction and death. I, too, was deceived by the greatest deceiver of them all. If it had not been for my earlier years learning of Christ and learning how to pray, I know I wouldn't be here today to tell you about the plots Satan has for me and you. Especially for you! I say especially for you, because I have learned my lesson and will no longer give Satan any part of my life.

God has a better plan for your life, and as Satan told me, you should stay with God; he loves you. Those are words I will never forget as long as I live. Even the father of lies told the truth once. God loves us all and gave his life for us. He hears our prayers and answers them according to His will. I have been given another chance.

Many who travel this road will never return; their fates will be sealed forever. I was one of the ones who knew God could forgive and help me. I hoped I had not gone so far that I couldn't turn back or that I couldn't be forgiven. My only trust and hope were in God, and He didn't let me down. I have a long way to go, but I'm here for a reason: to be a witness to you of how much God loves us and, if we return to him, even when we're in trouble, he is ready to receive us back. No matter how far we've traveled on that road of destruction and death, if we confess our sins, he is faithful and he will forgive us our sins, and will cleanse us from all unrighteousness, 1 John chapter one verse nine. God keeps his promise, and I am living proof he will do it! Satan is not your friend. No matter how long you hang out, smoke, drink, party, drug, or live an immoral lifestyle with him, he will never be your friend. His only purpose is to make life seem so irresistible to you that you can't resist it, and then he destroys you; he is a master at his job; he's had thousands of years to practice, and we will never smart-outsmart him, out-think him, or deliver ourselves from his firm hold on us. We are no match for him.

I cannot express how much of a deceiver he is; this is his whole purpose: to deceive and destroy. We must always stay within God's will; we cannot step outside the safety zone! Once you're out, you're fair game, and don't think for a moment you're not; I didn't realize how far out of the safety zone I had traveled until it was almost too late. Thank God I didn't die instantly; I was able to think back to my early upbringing about how I could ask for God's help in times of need or in times of trouble; he would hear from heaven, then answer my prayers, and how he could and would forgive if I asked and was sincere when I asked. I am a miracle; no longer will I allow Satan to use and abuse me.

I've chosen to rededicate my life to Christ and will serve only him from this day forward. After all, Satan was right about one thing: God does love me, and he loves you. Satan will never love us! It's not in his nature to love anyone.

No matter how long you serve him, he will never have your best interests at heart. Everything about him is a lie, and he is a deceiver;

you will never know it's him behind the mask. And what about all the people who do not know Christ? How do we let them know about the love God has for us? And about the plans that Satan has for them? How do we keep them from going down such a deadly road? They need to know, and if you have traveled this road as I have and were given another chance to help someone else not to make the same mistake, then we must tell them about the love of Christ, encourage them to study his word (The Bible), and to teach their children from an early age about the love of God.

We must be living examples, so they can see Christ through us and choose Jesus as their savior. Let's tell them so that Satan and his lies will destroy no more lives. I decided to tell everyone I come in contact with. What about you? When I think back on all that's happened to me in such a short time, the only thing that keeps coming back to my mind is:

Everything about him was perfect: his tall, dark body, kind words, pleasing-to-the-eye looks, and a smile to die for. He was perfect, one in two million! What woman wouldn't want him?

The funny thing was, my gut told me something different, and I should have listened!

www.ingramcontent.com/pod-product-compliance
Lightning Source LLC
Chambersburg PA
CBHW071102120626
46546CB00003B/1256